[*All Rights Reserved.*

THE OFFICIAL HISTORY

OF

THE RUSSO-JAPANESE WAR.

PART I.

SECOND EDITION.

PREPARED BY

THE HISTORICAL SECTION OF THE COMMITTEE
OF IMPERIAL DEFENCE.

The Naval & Military Press Ltd

Published by

The Naval & Military Press Ltd
Unit 5 Riverside, Brambleside
Bellbrook Industrial Estate
Uckfield, East Sussex
TN22 1QQ England

Tel: +44 (0)1825 749494

www.naval-military-press.com
www.nmarchive.com

In reprinting in facsimile from the original, any imperfections are inevitably reproduced and the quality may fall short of modern type and cartographic standards.

(Wt. 19634—62 2000 11 | 09—H & S 4718)

TABLE OF CONTENTS.

	PAGE

CHAPTER I.
Political Events leading up to the Declaration of War ... 7

CHAPTER II.
The War Strength of Japan and Russia—The Japanese Army—The Russian Army—The Navies of the Two Powers ... 19

CHAPTER III.
The Theatre of War and Lines of Communication 36

CHAPTER IV.
The Opening of Hostilities 40

CHAPTER V.
The Landing of the Japanese First Army in Korea and the Concentration on the Ya-lu 45

CHAPTER VI.
The Battle of the Ya-lu 55

APPENDICES.

A. Strength of the Russian Troops in the Far East, *i.e.*, East of Lake Baikal, in February, 1904 79

B. (I.) Geographical Distribution of the Russian Forces in Manchuria (Exclusive of the Kuan-Tung Peninsula) at the End of April, 1904 83

B. (II.) Strength and Composition of the Russian Combatant Forces in the Far East at the End of April, 1904 (Exclusive of Fortress and Technical Troops) ... ...

C. Order of Battle of the First Japanese Army and Russian "Eastern Force" at the Battle of the Ya-lu—Losses ... 89

PLATE 1.

Northern Korea, the Advance of the Japanese First Army
to face p. 45

MAPS AT END

Strategical.

The Situation at the Beginning of February, 1904 ... Map 1

Tactical.

The Battle of the Ya-lu, 30th April, 1904 ... ... ,, I/1
The Battle of the Ya-lu, 1st May, 1904 ... ... ,, I/2

PREFACE.

As a considerable time must necessarily elapse before either of the combatants in the late campaign in Manchuria produces an official history of the operations, it has been thought advisable to prepare a narrative of which the present publication is the First Part.

This work, which has been compiled by the General Staff, lays no claim to be complete and accurate in every respect, but all available information, with the exception of such matter as it has been considered necessary to withhold, has been utilized.

Criticism has been excluded, as it is necessarily of doubtful value when based upon imperfect knowledge, and naval operations have only been touched upon in so far as they affect movements on land.

The Part, now published, deals with the causes of the war, and the opening events up to and including the battle of the Ya-lu. Other parts to complete the work will be issued from time to time.

General Staff,
 War Office.

August, 1906.

PREFACE TO SECOND EDITION.

THE necessity for producing a Second Edition of Part I. of the Official History of the Russo-Japanese War has afforded an opportunity of publishing such further information with regard to the opening phase of the campaign as has become available during the past three years. In all essential points the original work, as produced by the General Staff, remains unaltered; but our knowledge of the advance of the Japanese First Army through Korea, and of the details of the battle of the Ya-lu is now somewhat fuller than it was three years ago.

The chapter included in this volume will ultimately form part of the combined Naval and Military History which is in course of preparation, and until the appearance of the completed work all criticism is withheld, in accordance with the wishes of the General Staff.

 Committee of Imperial Defence.
  October, 1909.

THE OFFICIAL HISTORY OF THE RUSSO-JAPANESE WAR.

CHAPTER I.

POLITICAL EVENTS LEADING UP TO THE DECLARATION OF WAR.

ON the 14th November, 1860, six days after the withdrawal of the allied forces of Great Britain and France from Peking, a treaty of the highest importance was concluded between Russia and China, whereby the eastern coast of Manchuria from the Amur to the Korean frontier, a district which subsequently became known as the *Primorsk* or Maritime Province, was ceded to the Tsar. Nearly three centuries earlier, the Cossack Yermak, acting under imperial auspices, had led his motley band of freebooters across the Urals to subjugate Siberia, and the explorers who had followed in his footsteps now found themselves established on the far distant shores of the Sea of Japan.

The Russian advance to the Pacific.

The advance to the dreary confines of the Asiatic continent, though spasmodic, had been rapid; conquest had led to conquest, and the treaty signed at Peking marked one stage, but not the last, in the absorption of vast regions into the Russian Empire. Checked again and again in her efforts to reach the Mediterranean, Russia had followed the line of least resistance and, although it had led her far afield, she now possessed a frontier on the sea. The Peking treaty was a veritable triumph of Muscovite diplomacy, extracted as it was from the Chinese at a time when, smarting from the lesson lately taught them by the Allies, they were in no position to resist. But though Russia's eastern boundary was now washed by the same sea that half surrounds the empire of Japan, her aspirations were unsatisfied. Along the coast line of her new possessions no ice-free port existed, for Vladivostok at its southern extremity, whither the Russian naval Head-Quarters were moved from Nikolaievsk, is closed by ice for three months of the year.* Moreover, from that port admission to the Pacific mainly depended on the goodwill of Japan, for the two principal channels which lead to the open sea were practically in her hands.† On the

---

* A passage for naval vessels is now maintained by means of ice-breakers.
† See Strategical Map I.

north-east, between Yezo (Hokkaido) and the main island of Hondo, is the narrow Tsugaru channel, while on the south are the straits between the southern shore of Korea and the Japanese island of Kiushu or Nine Provinces. The northern route is under Japanese control, and in the southern straits, which measure little more than six score miles across, the islands of Tsushima and Ikishima are well situated for guarding the passage east and west.

The problem of securing freedom of navigation to and from Vladivostok through these straits, under all conditions, could not be satisfactorily solved by Russia unless she could obtain a foothold in Southern Korea, or could debar her island neighbour from acquiring one. The time was inopportune for further territorial expansion on the mainland, but there remained other means which would afford the necessary access to the ocean. The island of Tsushima, which possesses several good harbours, might be occupied and added to the Tsar's dominions; and, with this intention, a Russian warship landed a party of marines there in 1861. Remonstrances from the alarmed inhabitants proved of no avail, but on the appearance of a British squadron, backed by a protest from the British Minister at Yedo (Tokio), the intruders were withdrawn. Several years passed and no other attempt like that on Tsushima was made, but the necessity for an ice-free port was not lost sight of by the Russian government.

In 1885, the situation in the Far East revived interest in the question, and, with a view to securing a port which should be accessible throughout the year, Russia entered into negotiations for the lease of Port Lazarev in North-Eastern Korea. This project was subsequently abandoned, and Russia announced her intention " never to occupy Korean territory under any circumstances whatever." In the meantime the British government had occupied Port Hamilton, in the Korean Straits, but after the Russian declaration with regard to Korea, the island was again evacuated.

The gradual approach of Russia was viewed with apprehension in Japan. Many years prior to the incidents just mentioned, and before Russia had gained possession of the Maritime Province, her settlers in Kamchatka, striving to push southward, had given tokens of that spirit of aggression which culminated, in 1806, in depredations committed in the island of Yezo. Half a century later, differences which arose regarding the ownership of Saghalien reached a crisis and, although compounded at that time by a partition of the island, the weaker power found herself, in 1875, forced to give up the southern half, accepting in exchange what was practically her own—the Kurile group of islands.

The Russian acquisition of Saghalien.

The shame of this surrender, unavoidable though it was, sank deep into the hearts of the *Samurai*, and in the minds of Japanese statesmen the dread of Russia grew stronger. They knew that, in the past, China had proved unable to protect her own interests, and that though she posed as suzerain of Korea, whose north-east frontier was conterminous with that of Russia, the task of keeping that dependency inviolate was beyond her strength.

To avert the danger of a Russian occupation, partial or complete, two courses were now open to the Japanese. Either Korea, whose historic attitude was far from friendly, must be conquered, or, failing that, must be made independent. The first course, for which all preparations had been made, was abandoned, lest it should lead to outside interference and so defeat its object, and the alternative, which aimed at terminating the Chinese suzerainty, was chosen. To carry out the scheme all that was needed was the opportunity, and that was soon to come. In 1875, a few months after the decision to intervene had been formed, some Koreans opened fire upon a Japanese steamer which was fixing her position off the coast by soundings. Several sailors were killed, and the outrage served as a pretext for the opening of negotiations between Japan and Korea. In the terms of the treaty which resulted the suzerain power was studiously ignored, while the offending state was regarded as an independent power enjoying the same sovereign rights as Japan. But China, who was not to be rebuffed so easily, took measures to regain her former influence in Seoul, and in 1882 the moment came for furthering her schemes. In that year advantage was taken of an attempt to assassinate the Korean King and Queen to offer troops for their protection. The offer was accepted and Chinese influence was once again in the ascendant at Seoul. A few months after this incident Japan's turn came to reassert herself. The anti-foreign party at the Korean capital attacked and burned the Japanese legation, the minister escaping with difficulty to the coast. Reparation was demanded by the Tokio government and troops were sent to Seoul, where their presence, coupled with that of the Chinese garrison, caused disturbances and led to complications which threatened to bring on a war between Japan and China. But the danger passed and, in April 1885, an agreement, called the Tientsin Convention, was signed by Marquis Ito and Viceroy Li Hung-chang. According to its provisions, both countries agreed to withdraw their troops from Korea, and settled that if either power should ever find it necessary to intervene in that state with armed force, the other should receive due notice and should have the right to send an equal number of troops.

The Tientsin Convention.

By virtue of this convention, and in spite of constant friction between Korea and Japan, peace was preserved until 1894, when a wide-spread rebellion broke out against the government of the former country. The King's troops were defeated by the rebels, and the royal cause became so seriously imperilled that help from the suzerain power was earnestly besought. China complied with readiness and dispatched two thousand troops to Seoul, at the same time warning Japan of her action, under the terms of the Tientsin Convention. A Japanese mixed brigade was at once mobilized, and Fusan and Chemulpo were occupied. But the troops sent by China had already quelled the rising, and when she proposed a simultaneous evacuation Japan, tired of the continuous spectacle of misrule and resolved to terminate once and for all a situation which invited foreign aggression, intimated her unwillingness to withdraw until peace was placed upon an assured foundation. With this view she demanded, as a condition of evacuation, that certain reforms should be introduced into Korea. The Chinese government, however, peremptorily refused to admit her right to interfere and, after some negotiations which proved fruitless, hostilities began.

The campaign, which lasted eight months, opened with the battle of Pingyang on the 15th September, and two days later the Chinese fleet was dispersed in an engagement which took place off Hai-yung Tao, an island lying about seventy miles south-west of the mouth of the Ya-lu River. The Japanese First Army then advanced to invade Manchuria, and, forcing the passage of the Ya-lu on the 25th October, occupied the country as far north as Hai-cheng by the 13th December. Meanwhile the Japanese Second Army, disembarking on the 24th October on the southern coast of the Liao-tung Peninsula, captured Chin-chou on the 6th November, and on the 21st took Port Arthur by assault. Part of the Second Army then moved north, and on the 6th March, 1895, occupied Newchuang (Ying-kou), where it joined hands with the First Army from Hai-cheng. Three days later the combined forces attacked the Chinese, who had taken up a position in great force on the right bank of the Liao River at Tien-chuang-tai, and completely routed them. Prior to this decisive engagement, an expeditionary force had captured Wei-hai-wei in February. The Chinese, everywhere defeated, sued for an armistice, which was granted on the 30th March, and on the 10th April a treaty of peace was signed at Shimonoseki, in Japan. By its terms China recognized the "full and complete independence of Korea," ceded Formosa, the Pescadores, and the Liao-tung* Peninsular to Japan, and agreed to pay a war indemnity of 200,000,000 taels (£25,160,256). Pending the fulfilment of these stipulations, Wei-hai-wei was to remain in the hands of the Japanese.

The Chino-Japanese War of 1894-5.

The Treaty of Shimonoseki.

The significance of this treaty was not lost upon Russia, who realized that her whole scheme of expansion in eastern Asia was imperilled. With Japan installed securely in the Liao-tung Peninsula and exerting strong influence in Korea, all hope of possessing an ice-free port on the Pacific would disappear, while the possible dismemberment of China would be postponed indefinitely.

The intervention of Russia, France, and Germany.

So serious a crisis demanded instant action, and this took the form of a coalition between Russia, France, and Germany. On the 20th April, before the Shimonoseki Treaty had been ratified,

* The boundaries of the Liao-tung Peninsula are not clear, but the title seems to have included all the country south of line from Newchuang through Feng-huang-cheng to the Ya-lu.

the representatives of those three powers at Tokio presented a joint note to Japan, suggesting that she should forego her claim to territory on the mainland, since its retention would be prejudicial to the lasting peace of the Far East. Japan was in no position to meet so strong a combination and, simultaneously with the publication of the ratified treaty, an imperial rescript was issued, in which it was stated that the Emperor, out of regard for peace, "yielded to the dictates of magnanimity, and accepted the advice of the three Powers." As compensation for the retrocession of the Liao-tung Peninsula, Japan received from China 39,000,000 taels (£4,906,250).

Retrocession of the Liao-tung Peninsula.

A digression from the sequence of events in Far Eastern politics is necessary at this point, in order to glance at a project of great importance initiated some four years prior to the Chino-Japanese war.

The Trans-Siberian Railway.

For over thirty years the question of constructing a railway across Siberia had been under discussion in Russia, but it was not until the 19th May, 1891, that the first sod was turned by the Tzesarevich, now the reigning Emperor. The construction of this railway was pushed on with such energy from both the Asiatic and European termini, that five years later the eastern section had reached Khabarovsk and the western extended beyond Irkutsk to the shores of Lake Baikal, from the further side of which the line was carried on to Strietensk. The gap of about a thousand miles between Strietensk and Khabarovsk was still untouched, but the line across it was intended to follow the course of the River Amur, which forms the southern boundary of Russian territory in that part of eastern Asia. Unfortunately, that river makes a wide bend to the north, and a railway to Vladivostok through Russian territory must make a similar detour. But towards the end of 1896, a contract was concluded between the Chinese government and the Russo-Chinese bank, whereby the Chinese Eastern Railway Company was formed to construct a railway through Manchuria from Chita, some two hundred miles west of Strietensk, to a point on the southern section of the Ussuri railway between Vladivostok and Khabarovsk. By this contract the necessity for following the vagaries of the river Amur would be avoided and a direct and far more convenient line could be made to Vladivostok.

The Chinese Eastern Railway.

The next link in the chain of events which preceded the struggle between Russia and Japan was the murder of two German missionaries in the province of Shan-tung in the year 1897. This outrage was followed by prolonged negotiations which terminated, after several months, in the grant to Germany of a ninety-nine years' lease of territory on both sides of the entrance to Kiao-chao Bay, as well as a zone of influence and certain railway and mining rights. With Kiao-chao in German hands, Wei-hai-wei still held as a guarantee by the Japanese,

Kiao-chao leased to Germany.

and the prospect that Ta-lien-wan, owing to British representations, would shortly become a treaty port, Russia determined to settle the question of an ice-free port, and at the same time to establish her supremacy in the Far East. In December, 1897, her warships had appeared at Port Arthur, and on the 27th March of the following year a convention was concluded with China by which Port Arthur, Ta-lien-wan, and the adjacent waters were leased to Russia for twenty-five years, at the end of which period an extension might, by mutual agreement, be arranged. Other provisions included a neutral zone, and power to erect forts and other defences. Port Arthur and Ta-lien-wan were occupied on the 28th March, 1898, and in the spring of the ensuing year the construction of the southern branch of the Chinese Eastern Railway from Harbin to the extremity of the Liao-tung Peninsula was begun.

Port Arthur leased to Russia.

Immediately after the conclusion of this convention, a ninety-nine years' lease of certain territory adjacent to Hong-Kong was acquired by Great Britain, while Wei-hai-wei was also to be held by her, so long as the lease of Port Arthur to Russia lasted. The conventions granting these leases were signed at Peking on the 9th June and the 1st July, 1898, and Wei-hai-wei, which was still in the occupation of the Japanese pending the final payment of the Chinese war indemnity, was evacuated by them in favour of Great Britain. Earlier in the same year France had put forward a demand, which was granted on the 10th April, for the lease of Kuang-chou-wan.

Territory leased to Great Britain and France.

We now come to the two remaining stages of the prelude to the war—the Boxer rising and the Anglo-Japanese alliance. In 1899, the inflammatory edicts which were put in circulation, inciting the people to rebel against the powers whose aggressive action since the war with Japan threatened the dismemberment of the Chinese Empire, brought on the rising. First noticed during the previous year in the Shan-tung Province as a movement against native Christians, and next aimed at Chinamen displaying foreign sympathies, the agitation spread gradually over north China and became directed against all foreigners. Troops fraternized with the rioters they were sent to suppress, the chancellor of the Japanese legation and the German minister in Peking were murdered, and on the 12th June, 1900, the legations were attacked, and then besieged. Armed intervention on the part of the governments represented at the Chinese capital became necessary, and on the 14th August the legations were relieved.

The Boxer rising and attack on the Peking legations.

Prior to this outbreak steady progress had been made on both the Imperial Railway* and the Chinese Eastern Railway. In June, 1900, the former was running trains to Newchuang with a

---

* The Imperial Railway runs from Peking to Newchuang via Tientsin and Shan-hai-kuan.

break at the Ta-ling Ho, while the embankment of the line to Hsin-min-tun was completed. The Chinese Eastern Railway at the same time was running trains between Liao-yang and Port Arthur on an imperfectly ballasted road, and although through communication between Siberia and the termini at Vladivostok and Port Arthur was far from being established, the earth work had been completed, and considerable stretches of unballasted rails had been laid. Such was the position of affairs when the Boxer outbreak, spreading to Manchuria, forced Russia to intervene.

On the 5th July, the railway stations at Tieh-ling and Liao-yang were burnt, the Christian missions at Mukden were destroyed, and the French Roman Catholic bishop and his staff were massacred. The railway servants fled, protected by small Cossack escorts, some north to Harbin, others to Newchuang. On the 13th July, Chinese troops opened fire on the Russians from the bank of the River Amur in the neighbourhood of Helampo, and disturbances occurred elsewhere on the Russo-Manchurian frontier. On the 26th June, the Russian government issued orders for the mobilization of the troops in the Amur and Siberian Military Districts, and a few days later in the Liao-tung Peninsula. Troops were also despatched from Europe, and forces were collected at Vladivostok, Khabarovsk, Blagovie-schensk, Chita, and Port Arthur; but it was not until August that the Russians were in sufficient strength to cross the Amur and capture and burn Argun. At the same time seven flying columns were organized, composed of twenty-two and a-half squadrons of cavalry and thirty and a-half battalions of infantry, with ninety-six guns. These columns entered Manchuria from different points; three were to converge on Harbin, and two on Kirin, while the remaining two from Port Arthur were to operate in the south. Harbin, which was besieged, was relieved on the 3rd August and, by the middle of September, Hsin-cheng and Kuan-cheng-tzu were occupied, while Kirin was entered by a Russian column on the 23rd September. In the south, Mukden was occupied on the 30th September, by which date the whole country was practically in the hands of the Russians. Very little resistance had been met by them, their losses amounting only to two hundred and forty-two killed and twelve hundred and eighty-three wounded. Their forces in Manchuria were shortly afterwards reduced, the European units returning to Russia.

The Boxers in Manchuria.

Russian occupation of Manchuria.

Meanwhile the international contingents, which had relieved the Peking legations and occupied the province of Chih-li, had been gradually increased until they numbered about seventy thousand men. Negotiations were carried on between the several Powers and the Chinese government, and on the 16th January the latter agreed to the terms which had been demanded. The most important of these were the punishment of the principal authors of the outrages, an indemnity, control of the legation quarter, and the maintenance of Legation

The evacuation of Peking.

Guards, the razing of the forts at Taku and those which might impede free communication between Peking and the sea, as well as the garrisoning by foreign troops of certain points for the maintenance of that communication. At the same time the Powers agreed to withdraw their troops from Peking on the 17th September, 1901, leaving the Legation Guards, the total strength of which was fixed at two thousand men. The province of Chih-li was to be vacated five days later, but garrisons aggregating rather over six thousand men were to hold Tientsin, Shan-hai-kuan, and other places. By the end of August the contingents had been reduced to about eighteen thousand men, and during 1902 the numbers fell to the limit that had been arranged.

On the 30th January, 1902, the governments of Great Britain and Japan, " actuated solely by a desire to maintain the *status quo* and general peace in the extreme East, being moreover especially interested in maintaining the independence and territorial integrity of the Empire of China and the Empire of Korea, and in securing equal opportunities in those countries for the commerce and industry of all nations," signed an agreement which was to remain in force for five years. By it each power contracted, in the event of either of them becoming involved in war with a third power in defence of its interests in the extreme East, to maintain strict neutrality and use its efforts to prevent other powers from joining in hostilities against its ally ; but should any other power or powers join in hostilities, to come to the assistance of its ally and conduct the war in common.

The Anglo-Japanese agreement.

On the 16th March, 1902, a Franco-Russian declaration announced the satisfaction of the two governments to find in the Anglo-Japanese agreement the affirmation of the fundamental principles which they had themselves declared to form the basis of their policy, but reserved complete freedom of action as to the means to be adopted in the case of aggressive action on the part of a third power, or of the recurrence of disturbances in China.

Franco-Russian declaration.

This declaration was followed on the 8th April by the signing of a treaty between China and Russia, the text of which, when published in the Russian *Official Messenger* four days later, was accompanied with a fresh assurance that the government of the Tsar adhered to the principles of the integrity and independence of China. According to this treaty Russia consented to withdraw completely from Manchuria; while China, on her part, agreed to protect the railway as well as Russian subjects and their undertakings in that country. The evacuation was to be gradual and was to be completed in three successive periods of six months, or eighteen months in all from the date of the signature of the agreement, and during each period a stipulated section of territory would be handed back to China. In the following October, at the end of the first six months, the evacuation began, and the south-

Russian undertaking to evacuate Manchuria.

west portion of the Mukden Province was restored. The withdrawal from the second section was not, however, carried out on the date appointed. When the Chinese minister made inquiries at St. Petersburg, he was informed that the delay was temporary and that the Emperor's commands would be fulfilled; subsequently, however, the Russian chargé d'affaires at Peking presented a demand for further concessions regarding Manchuria. These demands, which were seven in number, were in general terms as follows :—(1) None of the territory restored to China was to be leased or sold to any other power; (2) the existing system of government in Mongolia was not to be altered; (3) no new ports or towns were to be opened in Manchuria without notice to Russia; (4) the authority of foreigners in the Chinese service was not to extend over affairs in Hei-lung-chiang, the northern province of Manchuria; (5) the Newchuang-Peking telegraph line was to be maintained; (6) on Newchuang being restored to China the customs' receipts were to continue to be paid into the Russo-Chinese bank; (7) the rights acquired by Russian subjects or foreign companies during the occupation were to be respected.

Russia's seven demands.

Protests from the representatives of Great Britain, the United States, and Japan were lodged against these demands, and on the 29th April the Chinese government finally intimated their refusal to comply with them.

Meanwhile events in Korea had aroused alarm in Japan. Although the Chino-Japanese war had settled the question of Chinese interference, there existed in Korea a strong anti-Japanese party which, headed by the Queen, opposed the party of reform, and created a general feeling of unrest throughout the country. During an attempt, made on the 8th October, 1895, by the King's father and some of the reformers to enter the palace for the purpose of presenting a plan of reform, the Queen was assassinated. On the 11th July, 1896, a rising in northern Korea induced the King to take refuge in the Russian legation, whence he issued an order which resulted in the murder of the prime minister and two of his colleagues in office. The Japanese government now appear to have accepted the Russian co-operation, for by a memorandum dated Seoul, 14th May, and an arrangement dated Moscow, 9th June, 1896, several possible causes of misunderstanding were removed, and it was eventually agreed to recommend the King to return to his palace, to employ liberal and moderate men as ministers, and to suppress all useless expenditure. It was arranged that Japan should retain three companies of infantry, to be replaced as soon as possible by military police, to protect the Fusan–Seoul telegraph line, while companies not exceeding two hundred men each were to guard the Japanese settlements, two being stationed at Seoul, one at Fusan, and another at Gensan. Russia, on her side, was to maintain forces of similar strength for the protection of her legation and consulates.

Russian action in Korea.

By a further agreement of three articles, dated Tokio, 25th April, 1898, the two governments (1) definitely recognized the independence of Korea, and pledged themselves mutually to abstain from all direct interference in the internal affairs of that country; (2) agreed to take no measure in respect to the appointment of military instructors or provincial advisers, without previous mutual understanding; and (3) the Russian government agreed not to hinder the development of commercial and industrial relations between Japan and Korea.

In 1897, a Russo-Korean bank had been founded, and Russian subjects began to take considerable interest in land purchase and concessions. A year earlier a Russian merchant had secured the right, with a monopoly for twenty-five years, to cut timber on the Ya-lu and Tumen Rivers, but work was not begun upon the undertaking until April, 1903. Then Russian aggression, which had so far been limited to Manchuria, became noticeable in northern Korea, and advantage was taken of the timber concession to occupy Yongampo, at the mouth of the Ya-lu River, with Russian troops. Other acts followed from which it became apparent that Russia had little or no intention of adhering to her agreement with Japan.

The issues both in Korea and Manchuria had now reached a point where representations on the part of Japan were unavoidable. On the 28th July, 1903, her minister at St. Petersburg was instructed that it was considered that Russia, by the seven demands enumerated above, was consolidating rather than relaxing her hold on Manchuria, compelling the belief that she had abandoned her intention of retiring from that territory, while her increased activity on the Korean frontier was such as to raise doubts regarding the limit of her ambition; that the permanent occupation of Manchuria would create a condition of affairs prejudicial to the security and interests of Japan: that, from Manchuria, Russia would be a constant menace to the separate existence of the kingdom of Korea, where Japan possessed paramount political as well as commercial and industrial interests, which for her own security she was not prepared to surrender or to share with any other power. The minister was therefore authorized to intimate the readiness of his government to enter upon *pourparlers* with that of Russia, which, on being informed, accepted the suggestion. Thereupon a draft treaty, in which their proposals were set forth, was drawn up by the Tokio cabinet. This draft consisted of six articles, and was to the following effect:—

(1) A mutual agreement to respect the independence and territorial integrity of the Chinese and Korean empires.

(2) A reciprocal recognition of Japan's preponderating interests in Korea, and of Russia's special interests in railway enterprise in Manchuria; the right of Japan to take in Korea, and of Russia to take in Manchuria, such measures as might be necessary for the protection of their several interests, subject, however, to Article (1).

(3) A reciprocal undertaking not to impede the development of Japan's industrial and commercial activities in Korea, nor Russia's in Manchuria. Russia was to engage not to hinder the extension of the Korean railway into Manchuria.

(4) A reciprocal engagement that if either power found it necessary to take military measures for the protection of her interests as set forth in Article (2), the troops should not exceed the actual number required and should be recalled as soon as their mission was accomplished.

(5) A recognition on the part of Russia of the exclusive right of Japan to give advice and assistance in the interests of reform and good government in Korea, including any necessary military assistance.

(6) All previous agreements respecting Korea were to be abrogated.

This draft was presented at St. Petersburg on the 12th August, 1903. The Russian government consented to negotiate, but insisted upon Tokio being made the place of meeting. On the 3rd October, the Russian counter-proposals were presented to Japan. They omitted all reference to China and Manchuria except in Article (7), which stated that "Manchuria and its littoral [was] to be recognized by Japan as outside her sphere of interest." The territory of Korea north of the 39th parallel was proposed as a neutral zone; no part of the territory of Korea was to be used for "strategic purposes," nor were any military works, capable of menacing the freedom of navigation of the Straits of Korea, to be undertaken on its coasts. In general, the proposals of Japan with regard to Korea were accepted as the basis of negotiation, but by limiting the treaty to that country, except in one significant particular, restrictions were imposed upon Japan there, while Russia was left free to do as she pleased in Manchuria.

In the negotiations which followed between the 16th October, 1903, and the 13th January, 1904, six further drafts of agreement were exchanged. Japan accepted the proposal of a neutral zone, but with the limitation that it should extend to fifty kilometres on each side of the Ya-lu, and acceded to the demand that Manchuria should be considered outside her sphere of interest, provided that Russia gave a similar undertaking with regard to Korea. She further consented not to fortify the straits, but a reference to "strategic purposes" in the same article was expunged. Russia, however, continued to endeavour to exclude Manchuria from the agreement on the plea that that was "a question exclusively between Russia and China," and that although "Russia once took possession of Manchuria by right of conquest, nevertheless she is willing to restore it to China, but with certain guarantees assuring security to the enormous interests which Russia has in Manchuria. While China is still insisting on her refusal to give such guarantees, it is not possible for Russia to come to any agreement with a third power respecting Manchuria, as the question is exclusively between the two countries concerned."

On the 13th January, 1904, Japan replied for the last time, accepting the Russian proposal that she should regard Manchuria as being outside her sphere of influence, on condition of a similar engagement by Russia as regards Korea. In presenting the last draft to the Russian minister for foreign affairs, the Japanese minister was instructed to request an early reply; for it was known that Russia was actively engaged in endeavouring to improve her military and naval position, by sending reinforcements of men and ships to the Far East. No reply being received, the Japanese government decided, on the 4th February, to terminate the negotiations, and on the 6th the Japanese minister at St. Petersburg informed Count Lamsdorff that he had been directed to sever diplomatic relations and to withdraw from the Russian capital. On the 10th February, nearly forty-eight hours after the first shots had been fired at Chemulpo, both countries published formal declarations of war. On the 12th, China, at the instigation of the United States, made a declaration of neutrality, and proclamations of a similar nature were issued on the 9th and 11th by several of the great and lesser powers. On the 23rd February, an agreement was signed by Japan and Korea by which the former country guaranteed the independence and integrity of the latter, receiving in return permission to utilize certain places in Korea for military purposes. This agreement was followed a few days later by an intimation that Japan proposed to undertake the immediate construction of a railway from Seoul to Wiju, and on the 8th March some three thousand Japanese engineers arrived in Korea to prosecute the work.

CHAPTER II.

WAR STRENGTH OF JAPAN AND RUSSIA—THE JAPANESE ARMY—
THE RUSSIAN ARMY—THE NAVIES OF THE TWO POWERS.

THE system of conscription was introduced into Japan in 1871, but it was not put into full force throughout the empire until two years later. Up to 1868 feudalism had prevailed, under which each feudal lord or *Daimyo* supported as many retainers—*Samurai* or *Shizoku*—as his finances would permit; but the restoration of administrative power to the Emperor, which took place in that year, combined with the increasing danger of western aggression rendered necessary a radical change in the military system of the country. Patriotism and loyalty to the sovereign were to replace the narrower forms of duty to the feudal lord and readiness to die at his command. Clans and tribal groupings were to disappear, and the ancient loyalty, built up by a thousand years of war, was to be diverted into broader channels, and one supreme form of national sentiment—obedience to the dictates of the Emperor—evolved.

The Japanese Army.

The new order of things put an end to the domination of the *Samurai* and, although at first it was feared that the other classes of the people—farmers, artisans, and tradesmen—about to be included in the army might lack the military spirit, subsequent events completely justified the confidence of the reformers. Loyalty in the feudal days had not been confined to the fighting classes, and the paramount duty of fitting himself to defend his native soil roused the latent patriotic spirit in the breast of every Japanese.

In deciding to adapt her army to modern conditions Japan took what was best and most suited to her needs from European systems, and in the work of military regeneration she was from time to time aided by foreign officers. Ultimately, however, all outside assistance was dispensed with and selected officers were sent to Europe to complete their studies. On their return they received appointments in which the knowledge gained abroad could best be utilized and, in course of time, permeate the army. As a model for a general staff, that of Germany was taken, and a corps of highly-trained and able officers was created, to whose labours both at home and in the field the credit for many brilliant victories is largely due.

But however much indebted Japan may have been to external help in evolving the formidable military machine which she now possesses, she owes to no one that wonderful spirit of self-sacrifice which animates the heart of every man—soldier or sailor—and makes him feel it a privilege to give his life, if by that means the welfare of the nation may be advanced. The whole army is imbued with the strongest sense of duty. The officers of all ranks are devoted to their profession and are educated to a pitch as near perfection as it is possible to attain. The men are highly intelligent and, thanks to the simple and frugal life led by them from early childhood, are possessed of great endurance, boundless patience, and a marked capacity for fighting under difficulties.

Terms of service. Every Japanese between the ages of seventeen and forty who is physically fit is liable to serve either in the army or the navy. Military service does not, however, usually begin until a man has reached his twentieth year, although between the ages of seventeen and twenty voluntary enlistment is permitted.

At the outbreak of the war, military service* was divided into four categories:—

	Terms of Service Years.
(1) Standing army (*Jobi Hei-eki*) subdivided into—	
(a) Active army (*Gen-eki Hei-eki*)	3
(b) First reserve (*Yobi Hei-eki*)	4⅓
(2) Second reserve (*Kobi Hei-eki*)	5
(3) Conscript reserve (*Hoju Hei-eki*) subdivided into—	
First Term	7⅓
Second Term	1⅓

The men belonging to the second reserve were those who had completed their service in the standing army, and both they and the men of the first reserve were called out for periodical training. The first term of the conscript reserve consisted of those men who, although liable to conscription and medically fit, had drawn high numbers and had consequently escaped service with the colours; and the second term of those similarly liable and qualified, who had escaped not only service with the colours but also the lot of service with the first term. The men of the first term received a preliminary training of ninety days' drill, under regular officers, and a further training of sixty days during the second and fourth years of service; they were liable, however, like the German *ersatz reserve*, to be called up to fill vacancies in the standing and reserve armies. The men of the second term were untrained, and, after completing their period of purely nominal service, were passed into the second section of the national army.

* The military system which existed in Japan at the outbreak of the war has undergone no fundamental changes since its termination.

(4) National army (*Kokumin Hei-eki*) subdivided into—
   First section ⎫
   Second section ⎬ Formed of men up to forty years of age.

The first section consisted of men between twenty and forty years of age who had completed their service in the second reserve or in the first term of the conscript reserve. The second section consisted of all men between the ages of twenty and forty not belonging to other categories, and was quite untrained.

By an imperial ordinance dated the 29th September, 1904, which had retrospective effect, the liability to serve in the second reserve was increased from five to ten years; and the two terms of conscript reserve were amalgamated, and service in it was increased to twelve and one-third years.

The total number of youths annually available for enrolment exceeded 430,000, and over 60,000 were taken for service with the colours, while fully 130,000 were drafted into the *Hoju*. The exact number of men in the various categories in February, 1904, is not known, as the figures of the annual contingents have seldom been published, but it may be taken to be approximately as follows:—

Active army	180,000
First reserve	200,000
Second reserve	200,000
Trained conscript reserve	50,000
Trained men of the national army ..	220,000
Total	850,000 men
Untrained men liable for service in the conscript reserve	250,000
Untrained men available for service in the national army, based on the population of 46 millions in 1898	4,000,000 men.

When the five younger classes of the trained men of the national army, probably 120,000 in number, were transferred to the reserve army in September, 1904, by the imperial ordinance referred to above, there were available for field service some 750,000 men with 18,000 officers.

Organization. In 1904 the Japanese standing army consisted of thirteen divisions, namely, the Imperial Guard Division and twelve territorial divisions; and also of two cavalry brigades, two artillery brigades, and the garrisons of Formosa, North China, and of various fortresses, as well as certain guards in Korea.

For inspectional purposes, the twelve territorial divisions were grouped into three armies of four divisional districts each, but as this arrangement was departed from at the outbreak of the war, the division must be regarded as the real unit of Japanese organization. When mobilized, each division,* which is a unit complete in itself, consisted, in round numbers, of 11,400 rifles, 430 sabres, and 36

* For details of a mobilized division and a second reserve (*Kobi*) brigade, see note on page 35.

guns, 830 engineers, and 5,500 non-combatants. Each divisional district also provided on mobilization a second reserve brigade composed of two regiments of infantry, each regiment containing two battalions, in all some 3,500 men. In some of these districts mixed brigades were formed, composed of a second reserve brigade of two regiments of three battalions, three batteries of field artillery, a company of engineers and a few troopers as orderlies, the whole amounting to some 5,000 men.

Depot units were also organized, each infantry regiment forming a battalion, each cavalry regiment a squadron, each artillery regiment a battery, to keep its own regiment and the affiliated *Kobi* unit up to strength.

Line of communication troops for each division were at first furnished by the *Kobi*, and afterwards by the depot troops, who were thus close at hand to replace casualties, and were themselves kept up to strength by drafts from the depots in Japan, where fresh units were continually being formed for training.

Each cavalry brigade consisted of two regiments; and in each regiment were four squadrons. The total number of sabres in the two brigades amounted to 2,300.

The two artillery brigades, each of three regiments, had a total of 180 guns.*

The garrison of Formosa, which was replaced by reserve troops, consisted of three mixed brigades, making a total of eleven battalions, three squadrons, eleven batteries, and three engineer companies or, in round numbers, 11,000 rifles, 430 sabres, and 66 guns.

The Japanese troops in Korea, kept as guards for the foreign quarters under agreement with Russia, consisted of two companies of infantry at Seoul, one company at Fusan, and one at Gensan, total 800 men,† and there were also small posts of military police, totalling 200 men, along the Japanese telegraph lines.

The field troops available were therefore approximately:—

	Rifles.	Sabres.	Guns.	Engineers.
13 divisions	148,200	5,590	456	10,790
13 *Kobi* brigades‡	45,500	—	78	—
Depot troops	52,000	2,600	78	2,990
2 cavalry brigades	—	2,300	—	—
2 artillery brigades	—	—	216	—
Formosa garrison	11,000	433	66	690
Guards, etc., in Korea	1,000	—	—	—
Total	257,700	10,923	894	14,470

* The regiments of the 1st Artillery Brigade was composed of three battalions, each with three batteries; the regiments of the 2nd Artillery Brigade had two battalions, each with two batteries only.

† These troops belonged to the 3rd Battalion of the 37th Regiment of the 4th Division.

‡ The figures in this line represent the strength in men and guns of thirteen normal *Kobi* brigades.

In addition some 400,000 trained men were available to replace casualties.

Four more divisions—the 13th, 14th, 15th, and 16th—were formed during 1904, as well as a similar number of *Kobi* brigades, raising the total number of divisions and *Kobi* brigades to seventeen, including the Guard Division and its *Kobi* brigade. Beyond these units no new formations were created during the war, and the recruits and reservists called to the depots were used exclusively to keep the original units up to strength. At first none but men with at least a year's training were sent to the front as combatants, but at a later period of the war it was found that the term of instruction could be reduced without detriment to six months.

Tactical training.

The system of training in force in Japan prior to the war closely resembled that of Germany, and the text-books of instruction were based on those of the latter country.

The cavalry, like that of European nations, was trained principally for shock action, but was also taught to fight on foot. The men were selected from among the most intelligent and best suited for this arm of the service, but they were indifferent riders, and their horses were overweighted.

The artillery was trained to open an action, and to work with the battalion of three batteries as a unit wherever ground admitted. Isolated action on the part of batteries was regarded with disfavour and as only to be employed in hilly or broken country where space would necessarily be limited. Great stress was laid upon the importance of concealing guns from view and fire, and earthworks were ordered to be made whenever possible.

The infantry was taught that the great object of the attack was to obtain superiority of fire; that the aim of every man must be to press forward regardless of loss, and that any wavering or lack of dash would lead to increased casualties and diminish the prospects of success. It was laid down that the deployment would be made under cover of artillery, and the troops pushed as close to the enemy's position before opening fire as the nature of the ground admitted. The difficulty of crossing the fire-swept zone by day was recognized, and much time was devoted to night operations. The distinguishing feature of the attack lay in the rapidity with which the men moved from point to point; at the same time the operation was characterized by deliberation, and the importance of reconnaissance and of entrenching was borne in mind.

Armament and equipment.

The cavalry was armed with swords, and the 1900 pattern carbine, taking the same cartridge as the rifle, was slung on the back. In the field the amount of ammunition was increased and ninety rounds were carried by each man. With each cavalry brigade was a battery of six Hotchkiss machine guns.

Five of the infantry divisions, the Guard Division, the four additional divisions, and the two artillery brigades were armed with the Arisaka field gun, which is not a quick-firing gun. It has a calibre of 2·95-in., a muzzle velocity of 1,600 f.s., and throws either a shrapnel shell of 13·23 lbs. in weight or a high explosive shell weighing 13·45 lbs. to a range of 5,000 yards. Six of the divisions had mountain guns of the same calibre as the field artillery, and these, though of less range, proved most effective. One division, the 7th, had two batteries of field and two of mountain guns. In addition to the field and mountain guns some batteries of howitzers of 4·72-in. calibre were used as army artillery.

The infantry was armed with the 1900 pattern of rifle and bayonet. The rifle had a calibre of ·256-in. and a muzzle velocity of 2,300 f.s., and was sighted up to 2,000 metres (2,187 yards). The ammunition was made up in clips of five rounds, and each man had one hundred and twenty rounds in pouches and thirty in the haversack, while an additional sixty rounds were carried in the battalion transport. The number of rounds taken into action was on an average two hundred, but was sometimes increased to three hundred and eighty.

Kits were carried in knapsacks with the greatcoat and shelter-tent rolled outside. Two-thirds of the men carried an entrenching tool strapped to the knapsack, in which, in addition to necessaries, were two days' rations; the whole weighed some 57 lbs.

An important item of the soldier's kit was the blue cloth holdall. This took the form of a sack six feet six inches long, but with both ends open, and was eight and a-half inches across when laid flat. It was made of stout blue drill, and was sewn across the centre so as to form two long compartments. It was used by men, such as those of the train, who were not provided with knapsacks, to carry their kit. With the infantry soldier, however, it served to carry ammunition in one compartment and emergency rations in the other. It was usually carried empty, but when it was known that a severe action was impending, the knapsack and its contents were discarded, the emergency rations were transferred to one of the compartments of the blue holdall, and as much as two hundred and thirty rounds were sometimes placed in the other compartment. The sack was then worn over the right shoulder *en bandoulière* by tying the two ends across the chest. This equipment was improvised owing to the necessity of carrying as much ammunition as possible into action.

At the beginning of the war the infantry had no machine guns, but during the autumn of 1904 ten of these weapons of Hotchkiss pattern were supplied to each division, and before March of the following year, this number was increased to fourteen, which were organized in two batteries, each of six guns, and one section of two guns.

The bridging section of each engineer battalion had sufficient material for a bridge one hundred and fifty-three yards long; and there were some thirty-five miles of air line and cable with each telegraph company.

In Russia, as in Japan, the motive spirit of the army lies in the devotion of the soldiers to their ruler. This almost amounts to a religion, and embodies everything which in other countries is understood as patriotism. The Russian soldier, coming mostly from the peasant class, is no stranger to a hard, laborious, and frugal life and it is not to be wondered at that he bears privation and endures discomfort without a murmur. The dull surroundings of his village home deaden his imagination and produce a stolid nature which, even after frequent defeats, is usually proof against sudden panic or disorganization. His natural submissiveness makes him obedient and respectful to his superiors, but limited education, and wits dulled by a purely agricultural life, give to his mind a superstitious and fatalistic bent. Brave and well-disciplined, he is steady under fire, and when well led is a very formidable enemy, possessing many admirable military qualities, both actual and potential. His officers, like himself, are brave, and form a body of men of the most varying degrees of education and social standing. The officers of the general staff, the majority of whom are graduates of the staff college, are well educated and obtain rapid advancement.

The Russian Army.

The period of military service in the Russian army extends from the twenty-first to the forty-third year of a man's age, of which the first eighteen years are passed in the standing army and its reserve, the remainder in the *Opolchenie* or national militia. Service with the colours lasts for five years, and in the reserve for thirteen years, during which every man is liable to two trainings of six weeks each. The actual time, however, with the colours is four years,* as he is then sent to the reserve. During the first seven years of his reserve service he belongs to the 1st Category, and is then passed into the 2nd Category.

Terms of service.

The national militia comprises all men fit to bear arms from their twenty-first to the end of their forty-third year, and is divided into two *bans*.

The Cossacks, the inhabitants of Finland, and the Christian native population of the Caucasus serve under special regulations. Muhammadans pay a tax instead of serving personally, but are allowed to volunteer for service in certain cases.

Organization.

The total number of trained men at Russia's disposal at the beginning of 1904 was as follows:—

Active army	1,100,000
Reserve of active army	2,400,000
Cossack troops	345,000
Caucasian native troops	12,000
National militia	684,000
Total	4,541,000 men.

---

* Since the conclusion of the war with Japan, colour service for the infantry and field artillery has been reduced to three years, and in the case of other arms to four years; service in the reserve being fifteen and thirteen years respectively.

For war purposes the army is classified as follows :—

Field troops (part of which are styled "reserve" troops and are so organized as to expand upon mobilization), depot troops, fortress troops, local troops, and national militia.

The field troops comprise the units of the standing army brought up to war strength by means of the reserve, and reserve units expanded upon mobilization.

The depot troops are formed upon cadres detached from the standing army, and are filled up by men not required for the mobilization of the active army, by recruits, etc. They serve to feed the field and fortress troops in time of war.

The fortress and local troops are completed to war strength in the same manner as the field troops. In war they are used for garrison work only.

The national militia in war time forms independent units for home defence, and may also be used to fill up gaps among the field troops.

The standing army at the commencement of 1904 consisted of the following units :—

(a) In European Russia and the Caucasus, twenty-five army corps.
(b) In Turkistan, two Turkistan army corps.
(c) In Eastern Siberia, two Siberian army corps.
(d) In various parts of the empire, a number of independent cavalry divisions and brigades, rifle brigades, and other troops not included in any army corps.

The composition of an army corps varies considerably, according to the part of the empire in which it is stationed. Thus in European Russia the normal army corps consists of :—

Two infantry divisions, each consisting of two brigades (each of two regiments of four battalions), one artillery brigade of six or eight batteries,* one sapper company, and administrative services.

One cavalry division of two brigades, each of two regiments of six squadrons, with two horse artillery batteries (twelve guns).

Corps engineers, consisting of one sapper company, one telegraph company, and half a pontoon battalion.

Administrative services, etc.

In round numbers, 28,000 rifles, 3,400 sabres, with 124 guns.

In Siberia infantry divisions did not exist at the beginning of the war,† and cavalry divisions were not included in the

---

* In every army corps one artillery brigade has 6, the other 8 batteries, making a total of 14 batteries or 112 guns, or 124 guns if the two horse batteries of the cavalry division be included.

† They were formed later by the expansion of the existing brigades.

army corps, which had also fewer guns than the European army corps. Altogether the organization of the Siberian army corps was of a provisional and defective nature, but, as the war went on, this gradually improved, and their number was increased from two to seven.

The composition of the various army corps which took part in the war, therefore, varied according to the part of the empire from which they were drawn; the various types and established strengths were as follows:—

(a) From the active army in European Russia, (the Ist, IVth, VIIIth, Xth, XVIth and XVIIth) Army Corps, each numbering 28,000 rifles and 112 guns. The XIXth, IXth, and XIIIth army corps were sent to Manchuria, but too late to take part in the war.

(b) From "reserve" units in European Russia the 5th and 6th Siberian Army Corps, each numbering 28,000 rifles and 96 guns. Of the 7th Siberian Army Corps (53rd and 71st Divisions), whose formation was approved by the Tsar on the 1st July, 1905, only the 71st Division* actually took part in the war.

(c) Expanded from Siberian "reserve" units, the (4th Siberian Army Corps), numbering 28,000 rifles and 64 guns.

(d) From East Siberian units, the 1st and 3rd Siberian Army Corps, each numbering 22,000 rifles and 64 guns.

(e) Lastly, the 2nd Siberian Army Corps was composed partly of East Siberian units and partly of Siberian "reserve" units, and numbered 27,000 rifles and 80 guns.

The cavalry, consisting almost entirely of Cossacks, was organized at the outset in separate divisions and brigades. No divisional or corps cavalry was provided for, but was detailed from cavalry divisions as required. The established strength of a cavalry division was, in round numbers, 3,400 sabres and lances, with, in some cases, twelve horse artillery guns.

About one hundred infantry depot battalions were formed during the war for the purpose of keeping the units at the front supplied with men. Of these, at least forty proceeded to the Far East, but the exact number is unknown. The other arms were supplied, partly by depot units formed in the Far East, partly from depots in European Russia, and partly by drafts of men serving with units in European Russia.

Fortress troops were stationed at Port Arthur, Vladivostok, Possiet Bay, and Nikolaievsk, and consisted of infantry, artillery, and engineer units. At Nikolaievsk was stationed a fortress infantry regiment of one battalion, which was subsequently increased to four battalions. The infantry portion of the garrisons of Port Arthur

---

* The 71st Division formed part of the 5th Siberian Army Corps, until replaced by the 61st Division.

and Vladivostok was supplied by four East Siberian rifle divisions, two to each fortress: each division comprised about eleven thousand rifles and from twenty-four to thirty-two guns. Two of these divisions had been converted from fortress infantry into rifles shortly before the war.

Troops for lines of communication were provided by independent battalions of Siberian infantry, Trans-Baikal Cossack infantry, Frontier Guards, and battalions of Siberian *Opolchenie*.

The Manchurian and Ussuri railways were worked entirely by railway battalions. Of these, six were East Siberian battalions, which were reinforced in the course of the war by several battalions brought from European Russia.

The system of tactical training was not unlike that of other European armies. Thus the cavalry was trained both for mounted and dismounted combat, but the musketry training necessary to make it efficient when on foot fell short of the requirements of modern warfare. The Cossacks, who formed the greater part of the Russian mounted force in Manchuria, were trained on lines similar to the regular cavalry, but did not attain to the standard laid down for the latter. Moreover, as the Cossack provides his own horse, uniform, and equipment for which he is inadequately compensated in case of loss or damage, he is naturally disinclined to expose them to greater risk than he need.

Tactical training.

In the Russian artillery the tactical unit at the beginning of the war was the brigade of two, three, or four batteries.* Indirect laying was little taught in peace time, but during the war it was much resorted to, and gun-pits were employed whenever circumstances permitted.

The infantry was trained in the belief that battles are won by movements in close order and by shock tactics rather than by the development of a well-aimed fire, and, although the regulations prescribed the usual attack formations, these were not closely followed. Extended order was disliked as tending to increase the difficulties of command, and to this fact is mainly due the heavy losses of the Russians in Manchuria as compared with those of the Japanese. A peculiarity of the Russian infantry soldier is that both in peace time and in the field he carries his bayonet fixed, and this, together with inadequate attention to rifle shooting, naturally inclined him to place his faith in cold steel rather than in bullets.

The cavalry was armed with sword, rifle, and bayonet, and although the Cossacks in Manchuria did not carry the last-named weapon the front rank of the majority of their regiments had the lance. The rifle was slung across the back and was practically identical with that carried by the infantry. Forty-five rounds of ammunition were carried by

Armament.

---

* The tactical unit is now the division of two or three batteries; two or three divisions form a brigade.

each man and twenty-four in the regimental transport. The Cossacks were indifferently mounted, but their ponies possessed great endurance.

The artillery was in course of rearmament when the war broke out, and there were several patterns of guns in Manchuria. At first only about one-third of the guns available were the new 3-in. Q.F. weapon, and in many of the batteries neither the officers nor the men had any knowledge of it; the remainder, with the exception of some batteries of mountain guns and howitzers, were guns of 3·42-in. calibre. The 3-in. Q.F. gun throws a shell weighing 13·6 lbs. to a distance of 6,000 yards, up to which range only the time fuze for shrapnel fire is graduated, while the older 3·42-in. pattern, although it has a heavier projectile, has a lesser range.

The infantry was armed with a rifle of ·299-in. calibre, sighted up to 3,000 yards, with a muzzle velocity of 2,000 f.s. The ammunition was made up in clips of five rounds; each man carried one hundred and twenty rounds,* and there were sixty-six rounds per man in the regimental carts. In Manchuria, each man carried fifteen additional rounds in his kit bag and a further supply in the pockets of his blouse, so that from two hundred to three hundred rounds were frequently taken into action.

Kits were carried in a waterproof canvas bag suspended over the right shoulder and hanging on the left side. In this bag were also two and a half days' biscuit and salt. The great coat was worn or rolled *en bandoulière* over the left shoulder, together with a portion of a shelter tent, and about eighty men in each company had spades. With extra ammunition, kettle, and other personal effects the weight carried amounted to about 70 lbs., or nearly 10 lbs. more than that laid down by regulation.

Machine gun detachments of four guns now form part of every infantry and rifle regiment of the line; but of those units which reached the seat of war before May, 1905, only five East Siberian rifle divisions, the divisions of six army corps, and five rifle brigades of the line were provided with machine gun companies. The weapon used was the Maxim automatic gun firing the infantry cartridge, and proved to be a great success.

Each pontoon battalion of engineers had sufficient material for a bridge which could be varied in length from two hundred and thirty-three to four hundred yards, according to whether it was required to carry siege artillery or the other arms; and the first and second companies of each sapper battalion had a light bridge park which was carried on six wagons.

European telegraph companies had forty miles of wire and cable, while East Siberian sapper units had four air-line sections, each section with about sixteen and a half miles of wire. There were also with the army in Manchuria three telegraph companies

---

* Thirty rounds in each of two pouches, 30 in a bandolier slung over the left shoulder, and 30 in a reserve pouch suspended by a strap over the right shoulder and fastened to the waistbelt on the left side.

with Marconi equipment for the purpose of maintaining communication between the commander-in-chief and commanders of armies.

The Russian forces in the Far East have always been subject to considerable variations in their organization and strength.

Russian forces in the Far East. Originally, a comparatively small force was maintained east of Lake Baikal, which sufficed for the garrisons of the frontier districts and of the Littoral Province, extending from the mouth of the Amur to Vladivostok. The strength of these troops, however, was gradually increased as the advent of the Siberian Railway and other considerations enhanced the importance of the vast region lying between Lake Baikal and the Pacific, an area which is known as the Russian Pri-Amur Military District. In the summer of 1900 the Boxer outbreak resulted in damage to large portions of the lines then under construction across Manchuria from Harbin to Vladivostok and Port Arthur. For the purpose of the campaign then undertaken by the Russians to re-establish their possession of the railway line, and to ensure its ultimate completion, the troops in the Far East were mobilized and reinforcements were brought from European Russia. In the middle of July the order to mobilize was issued, and in October the Russian troops, including those in the Kuan-tung District, numbered about 124,000 men.* In the middle of October, on demobilization, the Russian troops were reduced to forty battalions and twenty squadrons with seventy-four guns, or about 38,000 men, exclusive of the garrison of the Kuan-tung Peninsula, which numbered 14,600 men with 24 field guns. Four brigades of Frontier Guards, numbering 25,000 men, were then formed for the protection of the Chinese Eastern Railway.

In April, 1902, under the pledge given to China, the withdrawal of troops from the south-west portion of the province of Mukden as far as the Liao River, was put into execution; but some, at least, of the troops remained in Manchuria on the line of the railway. During the negotiations which immediately preceded the war, two infantry brigades,† with part of the divisional artillery, were moved from European Russia to Chita in Trans-Baikalia; two additional East Siberian rifle brigades‡ were formed by drafts from Russia and from the fortress infantry of Port Arthur and Vladivostok, and an additional railway battalion was raised, which reached Liao-yang early in September. Further reinforcements were contemplated, and various units in Russia

---

* Viz., in Manchuria, including the Kuan-tung District, 80 battalions, 62 squadrons, and 232 guns; and in the Pri-Amur District, 26 battalions, 25 squadrons, and 28 guns.

† *i.e.*, 2nd Brigades of the 31st and 35th Infantry Divisions, belonging to the Xth and XVIIth Army Corps respectively, each with 3 batteries of artillery.

‡ *i.e.*, 7th and 8th.

received orders to mobilize, or to hold themselves in readiness to do so, before the end of 1903.

It must not be forgotten that even the troops in the Far East* were scattered over the vast area stretching from Lake Baikal to Vladivostok, and from Port Arthur to Nikolaievsk; a large proportion of the force, therefore, cannot be considered as having been actually available for operations in the field at the opening of the campaign.

Although an organization of four army corps was officially adopted at the outset of the war, it was soon abandoned, for all practical purposes, by General Kuropatkin, and the troops were formed into armies and mixed columns or detachments, as circumstances required. The bulk of the Russian force available was massed in two main groups, in the neighbourhood of Vladivostok and Port Arthur respectively; a third and much smaller group was distributed over Southern Manchuria and along the railway between Harbin and Liao-yang, the latter of which places had been selected as the centre of the zone of concentration of the field army. The remaining troops were further north in Trans-Baikalia; some were on their way to the theatre of operations, but others were still in process of mobilization.

The disposition of the field troops was therefore as follows:—

(a) In the Ussuri District; *i.e.*, from Tsitsihar to the coast but north of the Vladivostok–Harbin–Tsitsihar Railway, in the fortress of Vladivostok, and near Possiet Bay—

Five East Siberian rifle brigades (1st, 2nd, 5th, 6th, and 8th†); less two regiments, the 5th and 18th East Siberian Rifle Regiments.

Two European Infantry brigades (of the 31st and 35th Infantry Divisions).

Two regiments of cavalry (the Primorsk Dragoon Regiment and the 1st Nerchinsk Trans-Baikal Cossack Regiment).

One sapper battalion (1st East Siberian).

Twelve field and two mountain batteries.‡

Total.—52 battalions, 12 squadrons, 4 engineer companies and 112 guns.

(b) In Port Arthur and Kuan-tung Peninsula:—

Three East Siberian rifle brigades (3rd, 4th, and 7th§) less two regiments (16th and 28th East Siberian Rifles).

One infantry regiment (5th East Siberian Rifles).

One regiment of cavalry (1st Verkhne-Udinsk Trans-Baikal Cossacks).

---

* See Appendix A and Strategical Map I for the strength and allocation of the Russian forces in the Far East in February, 1904.

† The 7th and 8th Brigades respectively had only recently been formed from the fortress infantry at Port Arthur and Vladivostok.

‡ One battery of the 2nd E.S.R. Artillery Brigade was in Port Arthur.

§ Formed on 14th February.

Two and a quarter sapper battalions (2nd and 3rd* East Siberian and one Kuan-tung Sapper Company).

Five field batteries.

Total.—25 battalions, 6 squadrons, 9 engineer companies and 40 guns.

(c) In southern Manchuria (*i.e.*, south of the Tsitsihar-Vladivostok Railway and exclusive of (b)—

One East Siberian rifle brigade (the 9th).†

Three infantry regiments (16th, 18th and 28th East Siberian Rifle Regiments).

Two regiments and five squadrons of cavalry (1st Chita, 1st Argun Trans-Baikal Cossack Regiments, and three squadrons of Amur and two squadrons of Ussuri Cossacks).

Two horse batteries.

Total.—19 battalions, 17 squadrons, and 12 guns.

(d) West of Tsitsihar and in Trans-Baikalia:—

One Siberian Reserve Infantry Brigade (4 battalions).

Four field batteries.

Total.—4 battalions and 32 guns.

The above table does not include the fortress and technical troops allotted to Nikolaievsk, Vladivostok, and Port Arthur respectively; these are enumerated in detail in Appendix A, and are shown on Strategical Map I.

Estimating the combatant strength of a battalion of infantry at 700 rifles, and that of a squadron at 120 sabres, the total number of Russian combatants in the field, exclusive of fortress and technical troops, may therefore be taken as:—

	Guns.	Combatants.
Infantry (100 battalions)	—	70,000
Cavalry (35 squadrons)	—	4,200
Artillery (25 batteries)—		
Field guns	168 ⎫	
Horse guns	12 ⎬	6,450
Mountain guns	16 ⎭	
Engineers (13 companies)	...	2,700
Grand total	196	83,350

During the war of 1894–95, the great superiority of Japan's sea forces enabled her at once to place her armies in advantageous positions, whence they overwhelmed China with ease and rapidity and soon compelled her to make peace. It was, therefore, natural that the important part which the command of the sea would play

---

* Formed on 14th February.

† At the beginning of February this brigade consisted of only 8 battalions, but the remaining 4 had been completed by the 18th February.

in the inevitable struggle should long have been foreseen by both Russia and Japan.

Naval strength of Japan and Russia in 1895. In April, 1895, the Japanese fleet was slightly inferior to the Russian naval force in the Far East, but by June, 1902, the position was greatly changed. A comparison of the naval strength of the two countries was then altogether in favour of Japan, a condition for which the slow rate of Russian shipbuilding was largely responsible.

During the next eighteen months the Russians worked hard to make up the ground they had lost, and, at the outbreak of war, as can be seen from the following table, there was not much to choose numerically between the fleets of the two belligerents.

THE NAVAL STRENGTH OF JAPAN AND RUSSIA IN FEBRUARY, 1904.

Class.	Russia.	Japan.
Battleships—		
First class	*Tzesarevich, Retvizan, Pobyeda, Peresvyet, Petropavlovsk, Poltava* and *Sevastopol*	*Mikasa, Asahi, Hatsuse, Shikishima, Yashima,* and *Fuji*
Second class	...	*Chin Yen*
Coast defence vessels	...	*Fuso* and *Heiyen*
Armoured cruisers	*Bayan, Gromoboi,* Rossiya** and *Rurik**	*Yakumo, Idzumo, Iwate, Tokiwa, Asama, Adzuma, Kasuga†* and *Nisshin†*
Cruisers—		
First class, protected	*Bogatuir,* Askold, Varyag, Diana* and *Pallada*	
Second class, protected	...	*Tsushima‡, Niitaka, Chitose, Kasagi, Takasago, Yoshino, Akitsushima, Hashidate, Matsushima, Itsukushima, Naniwa* and *Takachiho*
Third class, protected (19 knots and above)	*Novik* and *Boyarin*	*Chihaya, Suma, Akashi, Chiyoda* and four others of slow speed
Third class, unprotected (19 knots and above)		*Miyako, Yaeyama* and seven others of slow speed
Torpedo gunboats	*Gaidamak* and *Vsadnik*	*Tatsuta*
Destroyers	25 in number	19 in number
Sloops and gunboats	10 ,,	15 ,,
Torpedo boats—		
First class	10 ,,	58 ,,
Second class	7 ,,	27 ,,

* At Vladivostok.   † At Singapore, on passage to Japan.
‡ Under construction; joined main fleet in March.

Russia's effective fleet consisted, therefore, of seven battleships, eleven cruisers, five first class and two third class cruisers, twenty-five destroyers, ten first class and seven second class torpedo boats, and ten sloops and gunboats. This force was, however, by no means so formidable as it might appear at first sight, for it was lacking in many of the qualities which help to form a really efficient fighting unit. The battleships varied in speed, armament, protection, and tactical qualities. The same remark applies to the cruisers, of which four only were armoured, and of these the *Rossiya* and the *Rurik* carried their armaments practically unprotected. The five first class and the two third class cruisers were nominally of high speed, though it will be seen later that in some cases they had sadly deteriorated from their trial speeds. The destroyers were of various types, French, German, British, and Russian-built from British designs; moreover, four or five of those which had been sent out to Port Arthur in sections had not been completed in February, 1904, although they joined the fighting force later on. Lastly, the torpedo boats were old craft of slow speed and of little fighting value.

On the other hand Japan possessed six first class battleships and six first class armoured cruisers, most of which were of British design and formed two powerful homogeneous squadrons. She was also well provided with fast second and third class cruisers. Her nineteen destroyers, of which fifteen were built in England and four in Japan from British materials and designs, were of the British thirty-knot type; and of the fifty-eight first class torpedo boats, sixteen were quite new twenty-nine knot vessels, thirty-seven were modern craft of twenty-two to twenty-five knots, and only five were old boats. Of the twenty-seven second class torpedo boats, nine were new vessels of twenty to twenty-one knots, and sixteen, though ten years old, were in good order and possessed fair speed, eighteen to twenty knots. To these may be added twenty-six old cruisers, sloops, and gunboats which had no fighting value so long as there was a possibility of meeting the enemy at sea, but which proved invaluable for covering landing operations and for co-operating with the army when the command of the sea had been obtained.

In both the Russian and the Japanese navies service is compulsory, but in the latter there are many volunteers who engage for eight years' active service and four years in the reserve; in

Personnel of the rival fleets.

the former navy the term of service is ten years, of which, as a rule, seven years are passed in active service and three years in the first reserve. Theoretically, therefore, there should have been little to choose between the navies so far as concerned the efficiency of the personnel; but in actual fact it varied no less than that of the material, and here again a comparison is all in favour of Japan.

NOTE.

COMPOSITION OF A JAPANESE MOBILIZED DIVISION.

2 infantry brigades, each brigade of two regiments of three battalions.
1 cavalry regiment of three squadrons.
1 artillery regiment of two battalions of three batteries.*
1 engineer battalion of three companies with a bridging train.
1 telegraph company of three sections.
6 field hospitals.
5 ammunition columns (three artillery, two infantry).
4 supply columns.

In round numbers 11,400 rifles, 430 sabres and 36 guns, with staff, 830 engineers and 5,500 non-combatants.

COMPOSITION OF A SECOND RESERVE (*Kobi*) BRIGADE.

1 infantry brigade of two regiments, each regiment of two battalions.

In round numbers 3,500 infantry.

COMPOSITION OF A "MIXED" SECOND RESERVE (*Kobi*) BRIGADE.

1 infantry brigade of two regiments, each regiment of two battalions.
1 artillery battalion of three batteries.†
1 company of engineers.
A few troopers from the divisional cavalry regiment.
$\frac{1}{2}$ a divisional train.
1 supply column.
$\frac{1}{2}$ a bearer company.
1 or 2 field hospitals.
1 infantry ammunition column.
1 artillery ammunition column.

In round numbers 5,000 combatants and 18 guns.

* The Guard, 1st, 2nd, 3rd, 4th and 6th Divisions, were armed with field guns; the 5th, 8th, 9th, 10th, 11th, and 12th Divisions had mountain guns, and the 7th Division had only four 6-gun batteries, two of which had field and two mountain guns.
† The Guard "Mixed" (*Kobi*) Brigade had four field batteries.

CHAPTER III.

The Theatre of War and Lines of Communication.

The theatre of war, the scene of the struggle between Russia and Japan, may be divided into three sections, the sea, Korea, and Manchuria.

Of these sections the first and most extensive area was formed by the Sea of Japan and the Yellow Sea, two bodies of water linked together by the Straits of Korea. The former lies east of the peninsula of Korea, and from it the Pacific may be reached by several channels. The two most important have been already mentioned, and when war broke out they were practically under Japanese control; but a third way, free from ice throughout the year, leads to the ocean through the Straits of La Pérouse between the islands of Sakhalin and Hokkaido. Between the western coast-line of Korea and the Shan-tung Province of the Chinese Empire lies the Yellow Sea, at whose north-western extremity are the Gulfs of Pei-chih-li and of Liao-tung. To reach this portion of the sea the Straits of Pei-chih-li, some sixty miles in width, between the Liao-tung Peninsula and the Shan-tung Province must be traversed. On the northern coast of the Gulf of Liao-tung is the port of Newchuang (Ying-kou), which is closed for some months of the year by ice. It is situated on the left bank of the Liao Ho, about five miles from the mouth.

Thrust out from the province of Manchuria and stretching southward towards Japan is the peninsula of Korea. With a mean breadth of one hundred and fifty miles, it varies in length from four hundred to six hundred miles, and has an area approximately equal to that of England and Scotland. The peninsula is generally mountainous, and has been described as being "as plentifully sprinkled with mountains as a ploughed field with ridges"; nevertheless Korea is a purely agricultural country. It possesses many excellent ports, more especially on the southern and western coasts, while on the east the principal harbour is Gensan or Wensan. Situated on the Korean Straits is Masampo, a splendid landlocked port, and forty miles east of it is the Japanese settlement of Fusan where the railway* to Seoul, the capital, has it southern terminus.

Not far from the south-western extremity of the peninsula is Mokpo, and further north are the harbours of Chemulpo, the port of Seoul, and Chinampo. The former is connected with the capital

---

* This railway was completed in January, 1905.

by a single line of railway twenty-six miles in length. This harbour is not frozen over in winter, but there is enough ice to prevent the working of cargo during January and February, and to make it difficult from the beginning of December to the end of March. North of Chemulpo is Chinampo on the northern shore of the Pingyang Inlet, while some thirty miles to the north-east, on the Taitong River, is the important town of Pingyang, with 35,000 inhabitants. Chinampo is closed for at least two months annually by ice. The roads, or rather unmetalled tracks through the interior of the country, are of varying width and are generally steep and stony. In dry weather, cavalry, infantry, and mountain artillery can move freely, but in wet weather, or when the ground is thawing, movements are extremely difficult.

To the north-east of Korea is the Russian Maritime Province, and across the frontier line formed by the Ya-lu and Tumen Rivers lies Manchuria. The province of that name, which is called by the Chinese the Tung-san-sheng or "Three Eastern Provinces," occupies the north-eastern corner of the Chinese Empire. The area of the three provinces is some 366,000 square miles, but that of Feng-tien and Kirin, the actual scene of the operations which took place in Manchuria, is only 161,000 square miles, and is therefore slightly greater than the Transvaal and Orange River Colony combined.

Manchuria.

Within the province of Feng-tien, in the space between the Ya-lu and Liao Rivers, lies a confused mass of mountains whose main ridge stretches in one direction to the extremity of the Liao-tung Peninsula, and in the other far into the Primorsk, or Maritime Province, north of Vladivostok. In the neighbourhood of Hai-cheng and Liao-yang the range is known from its picturesquely pointed outline as the Chien Shan or Thousand Peaks. Several roads cross it, of which the most important is the Imperial Peking highway leading from Korea to the Chinese capital by way of Liao-yang. This road traverses the mountain chain by the Mo-tien Ling (the Heaven-reaching Pass), which is four thousand feet in height. Further towards the south-west, where the range is lower, there are several roads, notably those from Hsiu-yen and Feng-huang-cheng, to Hsi-mu-cheng and Hai-cheng, and still further in the same direction roads across the peninsula become numerous. The hills are for the most part wooded, more especially in the higher regions, and the roads across the main ridge are merely cart tracks, which make the passage of large bodies of troops and transport a slow and arduous affair.

West of the hilly region just described, a large area of the theatre of operations is occupied by the valley, or as it might more correctly be termed the plain, of the Liao Ho, where immense crops of millet and beans are grown. This millet or *kao-liang* (tall grain) is planted in drills two feet apart, and soon after it has sprouted the crop is thinned so that each plant remains about eighteen inches from the next. In the rainy season it grows rapidly to between twelve and fifteen feet in height, and thus forms an admirable screen behind which troops can manœuvre unobserved; but by breaking off the stalks some three feet from the ground this screen can readily be converted into a serious obstacle.

The Liao Ho, by which this fertile area is watered, enters Manchuria from Mongolia after a course of three hundred and fifty miles and flows into the sea near Newchuang. It is navigable at certain seasons of the year by junks of varying size, as is also its tributary the Tai-tzu Ho, which flows past Liao-yang and joins the main stream from the east. By an unwritten agreement, or mutual understanding, military operations were confined to the east bank of the Liao Ho throughout the greater part of the war, with the result that in the later stages the Japanese army was forcing the defences of a wide defile which was bounded by rugged mountains on the east and by a swampy river valley on the west.

The climate of Manchuria is temperate in summer, but in winter it is extremely cold. July and August are the hottest months, but the heat is not excessive. The rainy season generally occurs during these months, but occasionally the rains begin earlier and at times last into September. The rainfall although not great throughout the year, amounting usually only to some thirteen inches, is sometimes so heavy as to inundate the country and cause damage to the railway. The snowfall is light, only two or three storms, on an average, occurring in the course of the winter, but the snow melts quickly under the warm sun and does not lie for long upon the plains. The country is generally ice-bound from November to March, when the rivers, being frozen, are passable for heavy traffic. Roads in the European sense do not exist, being mere tracks through the soft soil, and after heavy rains or when the thaw begins they become impassable. The lack of good means of communication limits the period during which military operations can be carried on to the dry months of the spring, summer, and autumn, for the cold in winter is so severe that troops are practically driven at that time to resort to quarters in the numerous villages which are scattered here and there wherever there is cultivation; but in the hilly districts and in the north, where the population is sparse, they are few and far between.

To the west of Manchuria lies the neutral province of Mongolia, from which large quantities of cattle and ponies can be obtained.

To keep her army in the Far East supplied with troops and necessary war material, Russia was restricted to the Trans-Siberian Railway and its extension from the Manchurian frontier by Harbin to the south. The great length of this line of communication from Moscow to the extremity of the Liao-tung Peninsula, amounting almost to 5,500 miles, exercised an important influence on Russian strategy throughout the war, more especially during its earlier phases, and the difficulties were increased by the fact that the railway round the southern end of Lake Baikal was not completed for several months after the opening of the campaign.

On the other hand, Japan depended for the transport of her troops and their supplies upon her mercantile marine, which had risen from 167,000 gross tonnage in 1893 to 626,745 at the outbreak of war, and included in these figures were many fine and fast steamers exceeding 5,000 tons burthen. Hence, as soon as sea command was won, she could land her troops at almost any point on the seaboard of the theatre of war; and even before that object was achieved the southern ports of Korea, lying close to her own, were practically safe from the risk of Russian naval intervention. Moreover her strategic position was well suited for the assembly of a large fleet of transports, for her coast-line is studded with fine harbours connected with the garrisons in the interior of the country by rail, while the Inland Sea forms a practically safe line of communication as far as the western extremity of the main island, whence the distance across the straits to Masampo, on the southern coast of Korea, is about one hundred and twenty miles. The distance from Masampo by sea, to either Vladivostok or Port Arthur is rather more than five hundred miles.

CHAPTER IV.

The Opening of Hostilities.

ALTHOUGH Japan did not sever diplomatic relations with Russia until the 6th February, 1904, it had been evident to her for some time that little prospect of a peaceful settlement remained. Long before the rupture, her plan of action had been carefully thought out, and a wise division of her limited resources had brought both army and navy to such a footing, that, when the crisis came, it lay within her power to strike on sea and land without delay. Her naval strength, if slightly inferior on paper to the Russian fleet in Far Eastern waters, was rendered more than a match for it by superior efficiency. Her army, once sea command had been secured, could reach the field of operations in force superior to the Russian troops already there, and could, it was hoped, be maintained in greater numbers than those which the Trans-Siberian Railway could convey. The whole issue of the coming struggle, if the question of finance be excluded, evidently depended upon naval supremacy; but it was clear that no fleet, however powerful, could of itself expel the Russians from Manchuria, or bring the war to a successful conclusion. To that end the possession of an adequate land force was essential, but, despite her care and calculation, Japan failed to estimate correctly what its strength should be. The enemy's numbers in the field and power of adding to them, his preparations, armament, and general efficiency had all been searchingly examined; no efforts had been spared, no means neglected, to ensure a just appreciation of all that the struggle would demand; yet, such is the difficulty of forecasting with exactitude an adversary's strength, that, in the first year of the war, Japan was obliged to modify her military law in order to recall reservists who had been passed to the national army, and before the end of the campaign was forced to augment the permanent establishment of her military forces by four additional divisions. With a military system less elastic than that which she actually possessed, less well-fitted for the rapid training of both officers and men, her situation in Manchuria would have been precarious.

[marginal note: Japan and the command of the sea.]

As pointed out above, the leading object of the Japanese was to obtain command of the sea. For the time being, therefore, everything depended upon the efficiency of the peace organization of the two fleets, and upon being in a favourable position to strike the first blow. At the beginning of February, 1904, the main Japanese naval force, which was known as the Combined Fleet, was at Sasebo under Vice-Admiral Togo. On the same date the Russian fleet was distributed between several ports. At Vladivostok were the four first class cruisers *Rossiya*, *Rurik*, *Gromoboi*, and *Bogatuir*; at Chemulpo were the first class protected cruiser *Varyag*, the gunboat *Koreetz*, and the transport *Sungari*; at Newchuang was the gunboat *Sivuch*, and at Shanghai was the *Mandzhur*, also a gunboat. The strength of the detachment at Vladivostok was probably due to the congested state of the harbour at Port Arthur, where the main fleet was under the command of Vice-Admiral Stark, whose flag was in the *Petropavlovsk*. The junior flag officer was Rear-Admiral Prince Ukhtomski, with his flag in the *Peresvyet*; while the Vladivostok division was commanded by Rear-Admiral Baron Stakelberg.

Naval position of Russia, February, 1904.

In Japan, on the other hand, everything was ready for instant action. The situation was critical, and the consequences of a false move might have been serious. If the Russians could be anticipated in Korea, not only would Admiral Stark find it difficult, if not impossible, to secure a port in the south from which to operate against Japan, but the harbours on its western coast would be available as bases for Admiral Togo's fleet. But there was still another great advantage to be gained by a timely occupation of the peninsula. From Wiju on the Ya-lu to Fusan on the Korean Straits its length is some four hundred miles, and by laying hands on the capital and pressing quickly towards the Ya-lu, the northern ports might be secured for disembarking troops, and a long and toilsome march to the Manchurian frontier avoided.

Japanese attack upon Korea.

Rapidity of action was imperative, and, as mobilized troops could not be sent to occupy Seoul, four composite battalions from the 23rd Brigade,* at peace strength, were chosen for that service. The order for their movement reached them at 6 p.m. on the 5th February, and by 2 a.m. on the 6th, the day on which negotiations were broken off at St. Petersburg, they were embarking at Sasebo. Three transports, the *Tairen Maru*, *Haijo Maru*, and *Otara Maru*, which were lying in readiness, were employed. Two took the troops, numbering in all about 2,500 men, while the third vessel carried a temporary wharf, some boats, steam launches and other gear necessary to effect a rapid landing.

---

* Two battalions from Kokura, one battalion from Fukuoka, and one from Omura. These places are in the island of Kiushu, in which the naval base Sasebo is situated. Officers and men were drawn from all six battalions of the brigade.

Simultaneously with the instructions to the 12th Division, Admiral Togo was ordered to leave port on the following day and "to destroy the Russian fleet." At 1 a.m. on the 6th, the admirals and captains of the Combined Fleet assembled on board the *Mikasa*; the imperial message was read to them, and the remainder of the night was spent in discussing the war.

<small>Admiral Togo ordered to attack the Russian fleet.</small>

Admiral Togo's plans contemplated a torpedo attack on the Russian fleet which was known to have left the harbour and was believed still to be anchored in the roadstead outside Port Arthur. This attack was to be delivered by the whole of his destroyers on the night of the 8th, and was to be followed up the next morning by the armoured ships. The 3rd Division was to cover the destroyers' attack and was to ascertain, if possible, the amount of damage inflicted on the enemy. To Admiral Uriu and the 4th Division, with twelve torpedo boats, was entrusted the work of escorting the three transports and of landing the troops near Chemulpo.

At 9 a.m. on the 6th, amidst a scene of great enthusiasm, the five divisions of destroyers got under weigh and left Sasebo, followed by the 3rd Division and the torpedo boats, with their parent ships. During the forenoon the 2nd, 1st, and 4th Divisions also departed on their mission in the above order. The original plan appears to have been to land the troops at Asan Bay, but it was left to the discretion of Admiral Uriu to disembark them at Chemulpo, in accordance with the wishes of the military authorities, should he deem it feasible to do so. At 2 p.m. on the 6th February he left Sasebo. Outside the harbour he was joined by the three transports carrying the troops, and at 4.30 p.m. the next day he was off Single Island, where he met the battle fleet and was joined by the *Asama* from the 2nd Division, the *Akashi* and the 9th and 14th Torpedo Boat Flotillas. Thus reinforced he proceeded off Baker Island, where, at 8 a.m. on the 8th, he met the *Chiyoda*, which had left Chemulpo at midnight and was able to give him the latest news from that port. This vessel, to which had been entrusted the difficult and delicate task of watching the trend of affairs at Chemulpo during the last few weeks, reported that the *Varyag* and *Koreetz* were still lying in the anchorage, together with the following ships of other nations:— *Talbot*, British; *Pascal*, French; *Elba*, Italian; as well as the United States despatch vessel *Vicksburg*, somewhat further up the river.

At 12.30 p.m. Asan Bay was reached, and it was then decided that the landing should take place at Chemulpo. As the leading vessels approached the entrance to the river, the *Koreetz* was seen to be coming out. The Russian commander although quite unprepared for hostilities, then sent his men to quarters, and through a misunderstanding two shots, the first of the war, were fired by a light gun.* The *Koreetz* then returned to her anchorage near the *Varyag*.

* The commander of the *Koreetz* states that before the order to fire was given the Japanese had already discharged three torpedoes.

At 6.15 p.m., the troops began to disembark. By 3 a.m. on the 9th all were ashore, and fifteen hundred men were at once sent by rail to Seoul. The landing was effected in flat-bottomed sampans, which had been brought by the transports and each of which could carry about fifty men. At 6 a.m., all the Japanese cruisers, transports, and torpedo boats left the anchorage with the exception of the *Chiyoda*, which remained to deliver letters from Admiral Uriu to the various ships present. At 9.30 a.m., Captain Rudnev of the *Varyag* received a formal demand that he should leave the port before noon, and was informed that in case of refusal he would be attacked at anchor.

Troops landed at Chemulpo.

About 11 a.m., Admiral Uriu ordered his ships to take up their appointed stations and made preparations for carrying out his threat. Just at this moment the *Koreetz* was observed steaming out to sea followed by the *Varyag*. The action of Captain Rudnev was gallant, but his task was hopeless. An engagement took place about six miles from port. The *Koreetz* returned before she had suffered any serious injury, but the *Varyag* was very severely damaged. Both vessels succeeded in getting back to harbour where, to prevent them from falling into the hands of the enemy, they, as well as the transport *Sungari* were sunk after their crews had been transferred to neutral vessels.

Naval action at Chemulpo.

While Admiral Uriu had been engaged at Chemulpo events of greater moment had occurred elsewhere. By 6 p.m. on the 8th February, the main fleet under Admiral Togo was off Round Island, about sixty miles east of Port Arthur, and at 7 p.m. the destroyers were despatched to make their attack. The 1st, 2nd, and 3rd Flotillas of torpedo boat destroyers had orders to proceed to Port Arthur, and the 4th and 5th Flotillas were to make a simultaneous attack on any vessels which might be lying outside Dalny. Why the Japanese should have supposed that any portion of the Russian fleet would be found at the latter port is not known, but whatever hopes they may have had were doomed to disappointment, for the only vessel they found there was the British merchant steamer *Foo Chow*, which was anchored in the middle of the bay. Meanwhile the ten boats comprising the 1st, 2nd, and 3rd Japanese Destroyer Divisions left Round Island and steered for Port Arthur in single line. At 10.50 p.m., lights were sighted on the port bow, and were soon made out to belong to two Russian destroyers. These were the *Rastoropni* and *Bezstrashni*, which, in accordance with their orders, refrained from opening fire and returned to Port Arthur, where they were actually engaged in making their report at the time when the attack took place. However, their mere presence had some effect on the Japanese attack, for the leading destroyer turned to starboard to avoid them, and the rear boats, some of whom stopped to escape notice, became separated

The first attack on Port Arthur.

from the leaders. Thus, instead of being a combined effort by ten destroyers, the operation resolved itself into a series of attacks by groups.

The Russian fleet was taken by surprise, and in a few minutes the *Retvizan*, *Tzesarevich* and *Pallada* were struck by torpedoes. All three vessels remained afloat, and got under weigh as quickly as possible in order to reach shallow water. The *Pallada* grounded close to the lighthouse on the west side of the entrance ; the *Retvizan* and the *Tzesarevich* attempted to enter the harbour but both grounded in the gullet and there remained, leaving only a narrow passage on either side. By 2 a.m., all the hostile destroyers had drawn off and firing had ceased. At noon on the 9th the Japanese fleet came up, and attacked the enemy still at anchor near the entrance to Port Arthur. In this action four Russian cruisers were hit, but their injuries were slight and very soon repaired. After carrying out these operations, the success of which was greatly due to the secrecy maintained regarding plans and preparations, Admiral Togo assembled his fleet at Asan Bay.

Not content, however, with his achievements, he ordered another attack to be made on the Port Arthur squadron by destroyers. This was carried out with less success than on the previous occasion, for the night of the 14th February, on which it took place, was dark and stormy and snow was falling heavily. Two only out of eight destroyers found a vessel to attack, but these succeeded in damaging with torpedoes a third-class cruiser. Three days earlier another mishap had befallen the Russians, when the mine-laying vessel *Yenisei* struck a mine and foundered, losing ninety-six of her crew.

News of the activity of the Japanese in the Yellow Sea had meantime reached Vladivostok. On the 9th February, the four cruisers there and a transport put to sea, and on the 14th, while cruising in the vicinity of Hakodate on the Tsugaru Straits, they sank a small coasting steamer, but did not succeed in seriously hampering the over-sea communications of the Japanese.

CHAPTER V.

THE LANDING OF THE JAPANESE FIRST ARMY IN KOREA AND THE CONCENTRATION ON THE YA-LU.

ALTHOUGH Admiral Togo had not met with complete success he had done enough to render the transport of troops to Korea comparatively safe. For the present this was all that was asked of him, and no time was lost in dispatching troops to follow up the advantage which had been gained. The order to Admiral Togo "to destroy the Russian fleet" was issued on the 5th February. At 2 p.m. on the 6th, orders to mobilize were issued to the Guard, 2nd, and 12th Divisions, and to the fortresses of Tsushima and Hakodate; other forts being merely warned to be in readiness against attack. Apparently two alternative plans of campaign had been prepared, the choice between them being dependent upon the degree of success which the fleet might achieve during the first few hours of the war. If, as actually occurred, the Japanese fleet should establish its superiority from the outset, troops were to be sent at once to Asan Bay and to seize Chemulpo. If, however, the voyage should be considered too risky, the 12th Division was to land at Fusan, and thence to push forward to the Korean capital, distant about eighteen days' march. Along this road posts with food and other necessaries for the troops had been prepared, but the opening of the campaign had proved even more favourable to the Japanese than they had dared to anticipate. Chemulpo had been occupied almost without opposition, and it was now definitely decided to abandon any idea of marching on Seoul from the south. Chemulpo was to be utilized as a landing place, at least until the melting of the ice should open up some harbour further north, and the transports were ordered to equip at Ujina on the Inland Sea and thence to repair to Nagasaki. By the 14th February, the 12th Division had finished mobilizing and was brought by rail to Nagasaki, where it embarked in six groups. The leading group sailed at noon on the 15th, and, on the morning of the 17th, landed at Chemulpo; and by midnight on the 22nd the whole of that division, as well as the 16th and 28th Regiments of the 2nd Division and the 37th and 38th Regiments of the 4th Division, had

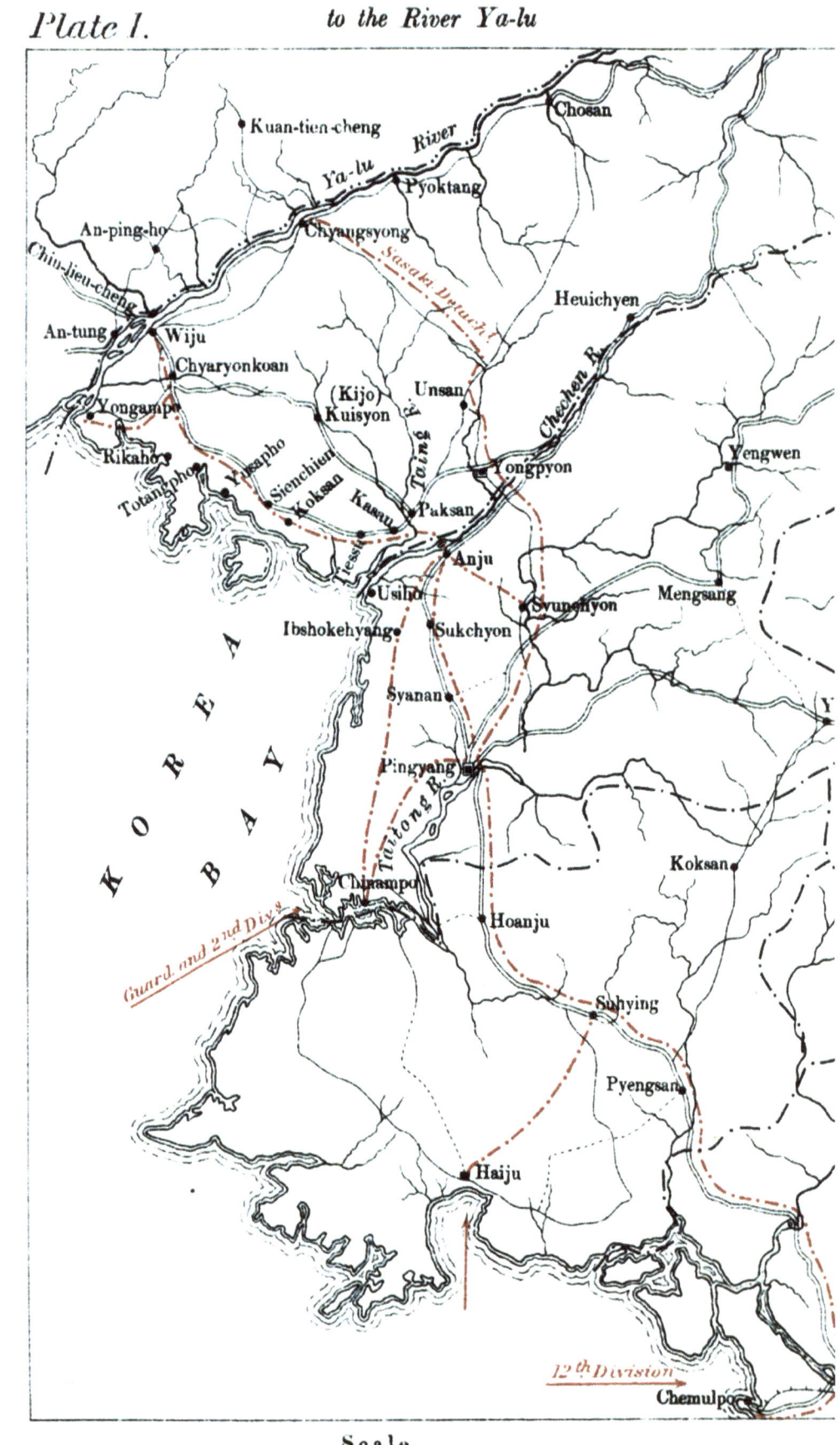

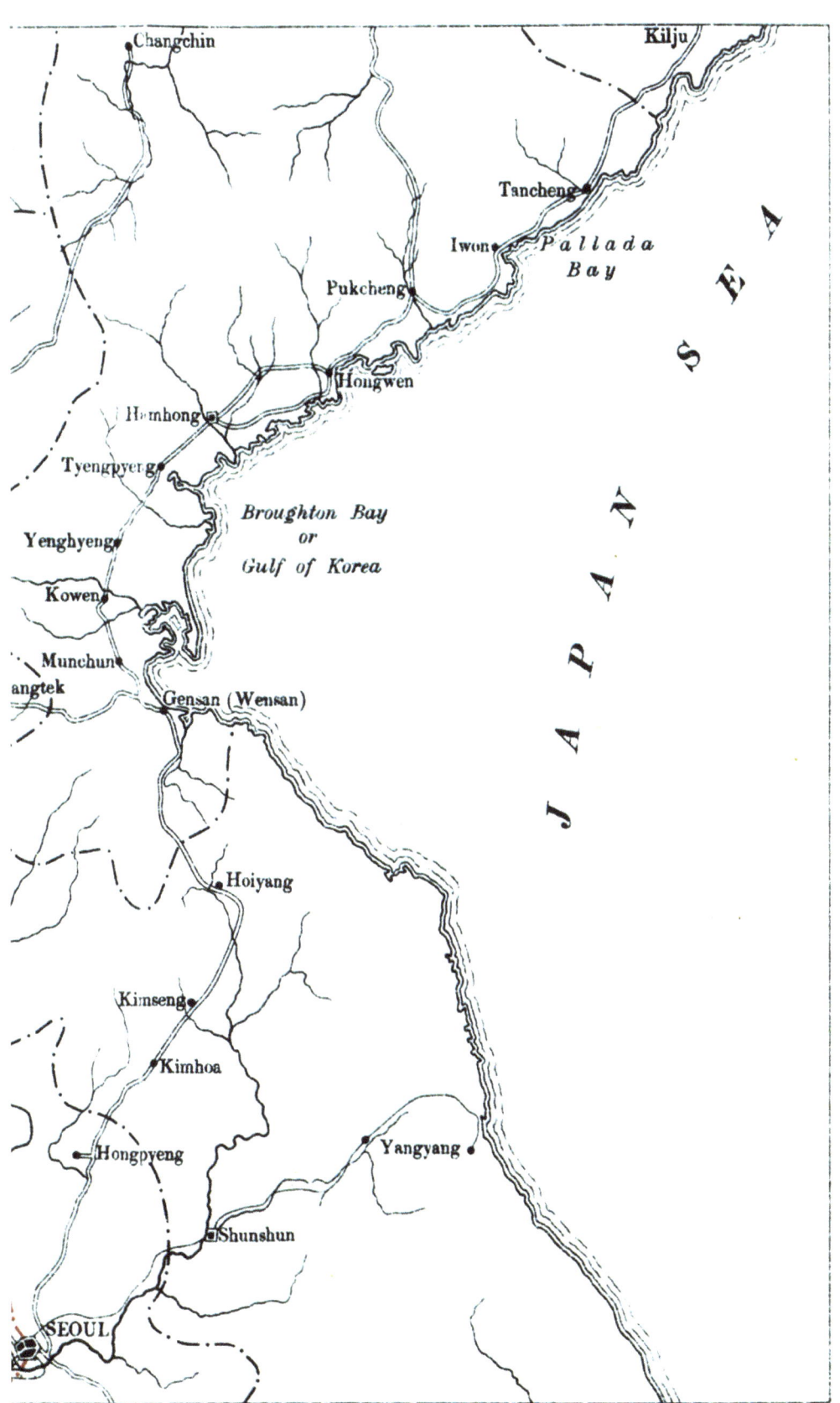

disembarked at that port. Thence they went to Seoul, while Fusan, Masampo and Gensan were all garrisoned by Japanese troops.

So far the Japanese land operations had been completely successful, and it was now decided to make every preparation for seizing a fresh base further north. As a preliminary step a company of infantry had been sent by sea to Haiju very soon after the first troops had landed at Chemulpo. From this company a party of twenty men with a commissariat officer was at once despatched to Pingyang, where it arrived on the 21st February, and at once drove off a small body of Cossacks who attempted to enter the town. Pingyang, the most important town in northern Korea, lies one hundred and fifty miles, or twelve days' march, north of Seoul. Since throughout the whole of this distance there were no supplies another company of infantry with a commissariat officer had been sent north from the capital, on the 15th, to prepare four line-of-communication posts. By means of this arrangement the cavalry of the 12th Division reached Pingyang from Seoul on the 23rd and assured the safety of the little garrison. On the 25th February the leading infantry of the division arrived, and by the 18th March most of it had moved north from Pingyang, leaving that place vacant for the reception of other troops shortly to arrive. Anju was occupied on the 10th March by two squadrons of Japanese cavalry, which were joined next day by a battalion of infantry; and about a week later three more battalions came up to strengthen the outpost line on the Chechen River, which at this time served as a boundary between the Russians and the Japanese.

Pingyang occupied.

Meanwhile mobilization had been proceeding steadily in Japan, and by the 4th March,* the Guard Division and the rest of the 2nd Division were concentrated at Hiroshima in readiness to embark. The sea at the mouth of the Taitong River, where the port of Chinampo is situated, though still reported to be frozen, would be clear of ice in a few days. From that point Pingyang could readily be reached, and the long march from Chemulpo through Seoul would be avoided. These advantages were held to outweigh any risks which would be incurred, and Chinampo was selected as the landing place for the remaining troops of the First Army. The movement of the transports by sea was to be covered by another naval attack on Port Arthur, and the disembarkation of the troops was to be protected by Rear-Admiral Hosoya with the 7th Division and a number of torpedo boats; while on land the same duty was to be performed by the troops of the 12th Division already at Pingyang. On the 8th a small party which had been sent to build piers at

Remainder of First Army landed at Chinampo.

---

* Both divisions are stated to have begun moving by rail to Hiroshima on the 15th February. The embarkation began on the 8th, but no troops seem actually to have sailed until a few days later.

Chinampo failed to effect a landing, though the ice was then melting fast; but on the 10th another effort was successful, and the news was telegraphed to Ujina,* the port of Hiroshima.

At this time General Kuroki, who had been appointed to command the Japanese First Army, was at Hiroshima and had received information that the enemy was concentrating near Liaoyang and Feng-huang-cheng, and that a small detachment of the 12th Division had occupied Pingyang, where the remainder was due to arrive by about the middle of March. Chinampo had been selected by the military authorities at Tokio as the point of disembarkation for the remainder of this army, but as the arrangements in Korea devolved upon him, General Kuroki decided to take measures lest the 12th Division should fail to reach Pingyang in time to cover the landing. The roads which ran from Chinampo to that place and northward along the coast were known to be bad, and would require repairs before troops, guns, and transport could move, and telegraphic communication from the landing place to the Head-Quarters of the 12th Division was also necessary.

General Kuroki therefore detailed an advanced force, consisting of the cavalry of the Guard and 2nd Divisions (six squadrons), a regiment of infantry, two battalions of engineers, and two telegraph companies, which landed at Chinampo on the 13th March. Of this force, the cavalry, one battalion of infantry, and one of engineers marched direct to Anju. That place was reached on the 18th, and the new arrivals raised the total force in its vicinity to eight squadrons of cavalry, five battalions of infantry, and one battalion of engineers. Immediately after the advanced force came the Guard and 2nd Divisions, dispatched in four groups from Ujina. The first group sailed on the 14th, and by the 29th the whole force had landed in Korea.

It is now time to turn to the Russians, who were gathering such troops as were available to oppose the Japanese advance and to cover the concentration of their principal army at Liaoyang. Towards the end of January, when the diplomatic relations between the two countries were highly strained, the 9th, 11th, and 12th East Siberian Rifle Regiments† had been withdrawn from Port Arthur and dispatched to the neighbourhood of Feng-huang-cheng under Major-General Kashtalinski. During the first days of February these three regiments were joined by the 10th East Siberian Rifle Regiment,† and the 3rd East Siberian Rifle Division was then complete and under its own commander.

Russian Mobilization.

On the 9th February, the day after the first attack on Port Arthur, the Viceroy Alexeiev issued a proclamation ordering the mobilization of the troops under his jurisdiction; on the 11th February similar orders were issued in the Siberian Military District; and on the

---

* Ujina is about 3½ miles from Hiroshima, and was the principal Japanese base throughout the war.

† At this time these regiments consisted of two battalions only.

15th the reservists were called up in the Departments of Viakta and Perm. On the 20th February, General Kuropatkin, who was generally regarded as one of the most able commanders in Europe, was appointed to command the military forces in Manchuria; on the 12th March he left St. Petersburg for the Far East, and reached Harbin on the 27th of that month. The mobilization arrangements in the Far East worked smoothly, but the units could not be brought up to their full strength without bringing men from Europe, and in the meanwhile the following steps were taken locally :—

(1) The formation of a 9th Brigade of East Siberian Rifles.
(2) The formation of a third battalion in each of the existing East Siberian Rifle Regiments.
(3) The grouping into divisions of the various East Siberian Rifle Brigades, and providing the necessary supply services.
(4) Providing the Siberian units with nineteen batteries of artillery, which were deficient.
(5) Furnishing the two European brigades with quick-firing artillery in place of the old pattern guns.
(6) The formation of a 3rd Siberian Army Corps by uniting the 3rd and 6th East Siberian Rifle Divisions.
(7) The creation of a Head-Quarter staff for the army of Manchuria.

The mobilization of the 2nd and 3rd Siberian Divisions, which formed the 4th Siberian Army Corps, was necessarily a slow process owing to the immense distances which the men had to cover before reaching their units. The mobilization of an infantry unit occupied from nineteen to forty-one days, of a Siberian Cossack regiment from eight to twenty-four days, and of an artillery group, *i.e.*, two batteries, from eighteen to fifty-one days. On the 9th April, a Caucasian cavalry brigade was mobilized, and this step was followed ten days later by calling up a division of Orenburg Cossacks and a brigade of Cossacks of the Ural.

Unlike her enemy, therefore, Russia was in no position to undertake military operations when her diplomatic relations were broken off, and the only troops available to interfere in any way with the Japanese movements were the 1st Argun, 1st Chita, and 1st Verkhne-Udinsk Regiments of Trans-Baikal Cossacks, all of which were under Major-General Mishchenko. On the 14th February, advanced parties of the Russian cavalry crossed the Ya-lu at Wiju and Chyangsyong, brushing aside a few Korean soldiers who were posted on the south side of the river, and protested against this infringement of their neutrality. On the 18th, the Chita Cossacks reached Sienchien, and one of the patrols captured a Japanese officer at Koksan. Still pushing south, some scouts under Lieutenant Lonchakov appeared in the neighbourhood of Pingyang on the 28th, and on the 2nd March there was a skirmish with the outposts of the Japanese 12th Division.

The appearance of the Russian cavalry led the Japanese to believe that some opposition might be encountered in the Anju valley. It was therefore thought advisable that the army should be kept concentrated, but, at the same time, for purposes of quartering, some dispersion of the troops was unavoidable. To reconcile these two requirements serviceable roads were almost indispensable; but, when the thaw set in soon after the middle of March, those which had been repaired by the engineers became so bad that marches were sometimes reduced to less than five miles a day. Guns, carriages, and transport carts sank to the axles in the mud, and men and horses floundered through with difficulty. In these circumstances the question of supply became acute, but was solved temporarily by employing ten thousand Korean coolies.

Such was the state of affairs when General Kuroki and his staff reached Chinampo on the 17th March. There he heard from a staff officer who had preceded him that it had been ascertained that, with the exception of fifteen hundred to two thousand cavalry between Wiju and Paksan, there were no hostile forces south of the Ya-lu. The weakness of the enemy now led General Kuroki to decide that it was unnecessary to await the concentration of his army* south of Anju before undertaking measures which would facilitate his eventual northward advance. Something might be attempted at once, and, with this view, he ordered the two rivers north of Anju, the Chechen and the Taing, to be bridged. To cover this work a force was detailed from Anju, consisting of seven squadrons of cavalry, two batteries of mountain artillery, and five battalions of infantry.† On the 25th, Paksan and Kasan were occupied, the enemy falling back upon the roads leading to Wiju and Unsan. By the 27th a pontoon bridge was thrown over the Taing, and another was built across the Chechen River with material which was obtained locally.

Advance of the Japanese First Army.

General Kuroki now wished to dispense with his covering force and to push forward with his main army after the retiring enemy. But the difficulties to be overcome were still great. A reconnaissance had shown that the main road along the coast was the only one fit for the movement of a large body of troops. Two other roads ran parallel to it, but between them and the coast road there was no lateral communication, while the front of the army if all these roads were used would be not less than forty-four miles. It was already almost impossible to feed General Asada's covering detachment, and it was quite evident that the whole army could

---

* The 12th Division did not at first form part of the First Army, but was placed under General Kuroki's orders on the 17th March, when he landed at Chinampo.

† 1st Guard Regiment, two battalions, 14th Regiment (12th Division), two mountain batteries (12th Division), the bulk of the cavalry of the Guard and 12th Divisions, one company Guard Engineers. The whole was under command of Major-General Asada.

not advance unless some fresh means of supplying it were devised. There was but one possible solution of the difficulty, namely, that the greater part of the army should march along the western road and should be supplied from a succession of depots on the coast. Combined naval and military reconnaissances were made as soon as the ice began to melt, and eventually Rikaho* was selected as the most favourable landing place south of the Ya-lu River. To cover the proposed depot the Asada detachment was to be pushed forward four days' march to Chyaryonkoan. Now, however, it was discovered that so large a force could not be supplied at such a distance from Head-Quarters even by allotting to it two-thirds of the regular transport of the whole army. The only course open to General Kuroki was to weaken his covering party, although by pushing up a small detachment so near to the enemy he was incurring considerable risk. Two battalions of infantry and the 12th Cavalry Regiment were therefore left at Paksan under General Imamura; and General Asada, with three battalions of infantry, two mountain batteries, and the 2nd Cavalry Regiment, was ordered to hold himself in readiness to advance as soon as his supplies could be brought round by sea from Chinampo.

<small>Supply depôts established on the coast of Korea.</small>

Meanwhile the Guard Cavalry, supported by a small force of infantry, engaged some six hundred Russian horsemen south of Tiessu, and occupied that place on the 28th with a loss of five killed and twelve wounded. This was the day on which General Kuroki had hoped to send forward the Asada detachment, but the necessary supplies did not reach the Chechen River until the 31st. Storms had occasioned considerable delays, and some anxiety was beginning to be felt as to the safety of the convoy, which consisted of Korean boats and was in charge of army officers, as no naval officers were available.

<small>Cavalry skirmish at Tiessu.</small>

At last all preparations were complete. The advanced party moved out from Kasan on the 1st April; on the 3rd, Chyaryonkoan was reached by the troops and the boats carrying the supplies arrived at Rikaho. On the day that General Asada began his advance, the 12th Division left Syunchyon, and on the 5th reached Tiessu, establishing depots, which were supplied by sea, at Yusapho, Totangpho, and Rikaho. On the same day also a flank guard of one regiment of infantry, a squadron of cavalry, and two mountain batteries under Major-General Sasaki was sent to Yongpyon to protect the right of the main army.

<small>Advance of General Asada.</small>

On the 4th April, General Asada's cavalry entered Wiju and Yongampo, and a general advance was at last considered feasible. It was to take place on the 7th, and on the night of the 5th General Kuroki issued his orders:—

<small>Occupation of Wiju and Yongampo.</small>

---

* This place is sometimes referred to as Ihoapho.

THE OCCUPATION OF WIJU.

General Kuroki's orders for general advance.

(1) The Asada detachment was to leave Chyaryonkoan on the 7th, to reach Wiju on the 8th, and to protect the front of the main army.
(2) The Sasaki detachment was to remain at Yongpyon until the 12th, guarding the right of the advance, and should then move to Chyangsyong on the Ya-lu, and reconnoitre towards Kuan-tien-cheng, Pyoktang, and Chosan.
(3) The 12th Division was to leave Tiessu on the 7th and to reach Wiju on the 12th, moving in two columns, with an interval of one day.
(4) The Guard Division was to leave Sukchyon on the 7th and to reach Wiju on the 15th, also moving in two columns.
(5) The 2nd Division to leave Ibshokchyang on the 11th, and to reach Wiju on the 19th.

The advance began on the 7th, and Wiju was entered on the 8th. On the morning of the 12th, a company of General Asada's infantry drove off an enterprising party of fifty Russians who tried to cross the Ya-lu near that town, but a violent storm which raged during the 8th and 9th put a stop to all movement for two days. On the latter date the bridge over the Taing River was swept away, and the columns of the Guard Division were separated. The bridge over the Chechen River barely escaped a similar fate, for its abutments were destroyed, and the centre portion was covered by two feet of rushing water. One half of the army was now completely cut off from the other, but, to prevent still further damage, engineers, helped by infantry and transport drivers, worked all night up to their necks in ice-cold water, and by piling heavy stones on the Chechen bridge saved it from destruction. Much damage was also done elsewhere. A bridge which had been made at Pingyang was swept away, the piers at Chinampo were broken, and all the newly finished telegraph lines thrown down in many places. Fortunately, however, amid so much to cause anxiety to General Kuroki, the landing stage at Rikaho stood fast and none of the vessels carrying supplies were lost.

Next day, the 10th, the water fell, but the pontoon company at Anju could not reach the Taing River until the bridge over the Chechen had been restored. By 7 a.m. on the 11th, a pontoon bridge was thrown across the former river and communication between the two columns of the Guard Division was again established, but the concentration was not completed until the 21st, when the troops of the Asada detachment rejoined their own divisions. On the 20th, the Sasaki detachment reached Chyangsyong from Yongpyon, after a trying march over difficult passes where all stores had to be carried by the men, and on the 26th the main army was strengthened by the arrival of five four-gun batteries of 4·7 in. howitzers which had been landed at Rikaho. These guns, which fired 46·3 lb. shells

Progress of the First Army.

filled with high explosives, had been purchased secretly just before the war. In places the road had to be specially strengthened with planks to facilitate their movement.

The 12th Division was now south-west of Wiju, the Guard Division was behind that town, and to the south-west of it stood the 2nd Division. From the date of the landing of the first troops of the Guard Division at Chinampo until the concentration of the First Army at Wiju, almost six weeks had elapsed, and in that time a distance amounting only to about one hundred and thirty miles had been covered. Nevertheless, when all the circumstances under which the advance was carried out are taken into consideration, it was far from slow. At first the climate rendered water carriage for supplies impossible; then, when that means became available through the disappearance of the ice, land communication, at any time bad in Korea, grew worse, and the three divisions of the army found themselves limited to a single road. Movement under such conditions is necessarily slow, and would have been more so had the Russians been able to offer serious opposition.

As it was, however, General Mishchenko had fallen back across the Ya-lu on the 3rd April, and had there joined the 3rd East Siberian Rifle Division under General Kashtalinski, whose force now consisted of eight battalions of infantry, twenty-three squadrons of cavalry,* twenty-four field guns, six horse artillery guns, eight mountain guns, and eight machine guns. These troops formed the nucleus of the Russian "Eastern Force," to the command of which Lieutenant-General Zasulich was appointed on the 12th April, and the units which were still required to raise it to full strength were hurried south as they became available.

<small>Concentration of the Russian "Eastern Force."</small>

On the 1st, 2nd, and 3rd April, the 22nd and 24th East Siberian Rifle Regiments and the 2nd and 3rd Batteries, 6th East Siberian Artillery Brigade left Liao-yang and reached Feng-huang-cheng on the 14th April. Thence they proceeded to the Ya-lu, except six companies of the 24th Regiment, which remained on the line of communication repairing roads.

On the 10th and 12th April, the newly formed third battalions of the 9th and 10th East Siberian Rifle Regiments left Liao-yang, and on the 24th April they arrived on the Ya-lu.

On the 13th, the 21st East Siberian Rifle Regiment, except one company which remained in the Pri-Amur District, and the 1st Battery, 6th East Siberian Artillery Brigade left Hai-cheng for Ta-ku-shan, and reached that place on the 21st April.

On the 14th and 16th April, the newly-formed third battalions

---

* As follows:—

1st Argun Trans-Baikal Cossack Regiment	6 squadrons
1st Chita Trans-Baikal Cossack Regiment	6 ,,
1st Verkhne-Udinsk Trans-Baikal Cossack Regiment	5 ,,
Ussuri Cossack Regiment	6 ,,

The 4th Squadron of the 1st Verkhne-Udinsk Regiment was in Port Arthur.

of the 11th and 12th East Siberian Rifle Regiments started from Liao-yang and arrived on the Ya-lu on the 25th and 26th April respectively.

On the 16th April, the 22nd East Siberian Rifle Regiment reached the Ya-lu.

On the 21st April, a mountain battery, escorted by a company of the 10th East Siberian Rifle Regiment left Feng-huang-cheng for Chang-tien-cheng, twenty-eight miles north-east of Wiju.

The Russian "Eastern Force" and the Japanese First Army were now face to face on the River Ya-lu, where they must be left for the present; for it is now necessary to glance at the general course of events elsewhere, especially at those operations in which the naval forces were concerned. On the 16th February, Admiral Makarov, a distinguished naval commander, left Kronstadt on appointment to supersede Admiral Stark at Port Arthur; and on the same date Admiral Alexeiev, the Viceroy of the Tsar in the Far East, proceeded from Port Arthur to Mukden, where he shortly afterwards established his Head-Quarters. Up to that time Admiral Alexeiev had controlled diplomatic relations between Russia in East Asia and the neighbouring countries, and had held supreme command of the naval and military forces there, but the probable magnitude of the coming operations required that their conduct should be delegated to others.

Summary of naval operations from the 16th February to the end of April.

On the 23rd, while the newly appointed naval Commander-in-Chief, Admiral Makarov, was on his way to Port Arthur, a gallant attempt was made by the Japanese fleet to block the entrance of that place with ballast-laden vessels, and so to prevent the Russian fleet, the greater part of which had been withdrawn to the inner roadstead, from issuing at will. A week later Vice-Admiral Kamamura with seven cruisers were dispatched to the vicinity of Vladivostok to try and bring to battle the four Russian vessels there. Information had been received that the latter vessels were engaged in operations connected with the land forces in that locality, but beyond bombarding the fortress at long range on the 7th March the Japanese squadron effected nothing.

On the 7th, too, Admiral Togo had put his fleet in motion and on the 10th, after an engagment between his destroyers and those of the Russians, bombarded Port Arthur. Thereafter the Japanese temporary naval base was shifted to a bay north of Chemulpo, whence the distance to Port Arthur was not more than about two hundred and forty miles. The naval operations were resumed on the 22nd March, when Port Arthur was subjected to a bombardment by two battleships from Pigeon Bay, and on the 27th a second attempt was made to block the entrance to the harbour. During the bombardment the enemy's ships gradually came out of harbour, as if inviting the Japanese to close and engage them under the fire of the forts. This procedure on their part, which was followed only after Admiral Makarov had assumed command on the 9th March, led Admiral Togo to conceive the idea of laying mechanical mines both east and west of the entrance to the harbour on the course over which the enemy's ships generally steamed. This plan was carried out on the night of the 12th April by a destroyer squadron, which joined the battle fleet before daybreak at a rendezvous a few miles from the port. At dawn the Japanese light cruiser division stood fairly close in to the entrance in order to lure the Russians across the minefield. The plan succeeded in some degree. The Russians came out and by good fortune escaped damage, but on the appearance of the Japanese battle squadron put their helms a-starboard and made for the entrance of Port Arthur. But their return was less fortunate, for the *Petropavlovsk* struck a mine and capsized, carrying down with her Admiral Makarov and some six hundred sailors. About the time that she disappeared, a second battleship, the *Pobyeda*, also struck a mine and was injured.

On the 15th, the bombardment of Port Arthur was repeated by the *Kasuga* and *Nisshin* from Pigeon Bay. For two hours fire was maintained by their guns, and the new forts at Lao-tieh Shan were silenced.

Ten days later an incident took place near Gensan. On the 22nd April, Vice-Admiral Kamamura had arrived at that place with a squadron of ten cruisers and other vessels which included two transports. On the 23rd, the squadron left for Vladivostok, and on the 25th, the transport *Kinshu Maru*, with a company of infantry on board, left the harbour apparently with the intention of landing troops at some point on the Korean coast. She was met, however, by three cruisers from Vladivostok which had evaded Admiral Kamamura's squadron, and was sunk by them. In this affair about one hundred men were killed or drowned and others, numbering some two hundred and fifty, were captured.

CHAPTER VI.

THE BATTLE OF THE YA-LU (MAPS I/1 AND I/2).

AFTER this slight digression into naval affairs, we must revert to the land operations on the River Ya-lu, where Lieutenant-General Zasulich was preparing to oppose the passage of the Japanese First Army. The position which had been taken up by the Russian commander extended from a point some four miles to the west of An-tung, through Chiu-lien-cheng to a bend on the Ai River a short distance beyond the Kuan-tien-cheng road. Opposite the centre at Chiu-lien-cheng the valley measures from three to four miles in width, and consists of a sandy plain broken up into many islands by the maze-like branches of the Ya-lu River and its tributary the Ai Ho. The ground in the valley is open and there is no cover except behind the patches of low trees and scrub which grow on the islands of Kintei and Oseki, or under the banks of the several channels of the river. That it was not intended to offer a very obstinate resistance to the crossing seems probable from the fact that the position covered a front of twenty miles, and that the high ground north of Wiju at the confluence of the rivers was merely held by an outpost. At that point is a rocky height called Tiger Hill, half a mile in length and five hundred feet high, which has the appearance of an isolated feature rising from the river bed, although in reality it is a southern offshoot from higher ground, with which it is connected by a col or neck. Posted on this hill artillery, up to the limit of its range, could frustrate any attempt to cross the valley except by night, while the same locality, if in the hands of the Japanese, would serve as a pivot from which to operate against either flank or the centre of the Russian position. Of this position only that portion which lies north of Chiu-lien-cheng was to be subjected to attack. Between that village and Ching-kou numerous spurs are thrown out towards the river from the high ground in rear, whence they drop steeply till they meet the valley, and usually terminate in knolls varying from one hundred and fifty to two hundred feet in height. At the foot of the spurs were infantry entrenchments, placed with a command of about twenty feet over the sandy plain in front. These works, which might easily have been made almost invisible by utilizing broken ground, were conspicuous at a distance to the naked eye, and consisted of breastworks revetted with boughs, with a trench in rear. Epaulments for twelve guns had been prepared on the high ground west of Chiu-lien-cheng but, like the infantry defences, they were not

The Ya-lu position.

concealed and moreover they lacked solidity. Lateral communications were difficult, and for guns were only possible along indifferent tracks, while the line of retreat was limited to a single road.*

The main strength of the position lay in its extensive field of fire, and in the obstacles afforded by the rivers in front of it. Of these rivers the Ai, which was ninety yards in breadth and rarely more than four or five feet deep, ran at a distance varying from three hundred to eight hundred yards from the Russian trenches. The Ya-lu flowed in two streams, both of which were unfordable. The southern channel averaged two hundred and thirty yards in breadth and the main stream three hundred and eighty yards.

The date upon which the attempt to force the passage of the rivers was to be made was selected so as to coincide as nearly as possible with the landing of the Second Army, whose intended movements were communicated to General Kuroki in the following message :—

"The Second Army will begin its landing at the mouth of the Ta-sha Ho† on the 1st May, and its disembarkation will take about forty-five days. The First Army will therefore advance as far as Tang-shan-cheng (midway between An-tung and Feng-huang-cheng) where it will entrench itself and wait until the Second Army has finished its disembarkation. The two armies will then co-operate." These instructions were received on the 17th April, and the Japanese, who had crossed the Ya-lu in face of the Chinese in 1894, were fully aware of the difficulties which had to be overcome. It was of the first importance that for the next ten days the strength of the attack should be concealed, and that the point of passage should be hidden from the Russian general in order that he might continue to maintain the wide front taken up by his troops. This object could only be accomplished by making feints by sea as well as on land, and by utilizing every artifice that ingenuity could devise. The advanced guard, as it approached Wiju, erected screens of *kao-liang* and trees at every point where the road passed over high ground south of the town. This precaution was necessary, because at those points the road was exposed to view from the right bank of the Ya-lu, and troops and guns could have been counted as they moved along it. On arriving near the Ya-lu, the three divisions‡ of General Kuroki's army were kept in the neighbourhood of Wiju, hidden in the low ground between the banks of the river and the heights to the south. To each division a section of the river bank was allotted for purposes of defence, and the sentry line, which was always kept concealed, ran along the left bank of the southern channel. No one was permitted to ascend the high ground on this bank, and the utmost care was exercised to hide all movements from the Russians.

* It would seem that a track leading through Liu-chia-kou to Feng-huang-cheng was also intended to be used.
† In the Kuan-tung Peninsula.
‡ For the order of battle of the Japanese First Army see Appendix C.

During this period also, the Sasaki detachment was recalled from Chyangsyong, but one battalion of infantry,* one squadron, and a mountain battery were left there as a flank guard to the army. The remainder of the detachment rejoined the 12th Division on the 29th April.

Russian troops on the Ya-lu. North of the Ya-lu, Lieutenant-General Zasulich had assumed command on the 22nd April, and on the 26th, in accordance with his orders, the Russian troops† were disposed as follows :—

At An-tung, under Major-General Kashtalinski—

2½ battalions of the 10th Regiment.
2 companies of the 24th Regiment.
1st/3rd and 2nd/3rd Batteries.
1 machine gun company.
Mounted scouts of the 9th, 10th, and 11th Regiments.

In all, approximately, 2,580 bayonets, 400 scouts, 16 field guns, and 8 machine guns.

At Chiu-lien-cheng, under Major-General Trusov—

12th Regiment.
22nd Regiment.
2nd/6th and 3rd/6th Batteries.
Mounted scouts of the 12th and 22nd Regiments.

In all, approximately, 5,200 bayonets, 240 scouts, and 16 guns.

At Tien-tzu, in reserve—

9th Regiment.
11th Regiment.
3rd/3rd Battery.

In all, approximately, 5,200 to 5,400 bayonets and 16 guns.

From An-ping-ho to Hsiao-pu-hsi-ho,‡ watching the left flank under Colonel Kartsev§—

6 squadrons of the 1st Argun Cossack Regiment.
5 squadrons of the Ussuri Cossack Regiment.‖
1 battalion of the 24th Regiment.
1 company of the 10th Regiment.
1 mountain battery.

In all, approximately, 1,250 sabres, 1,000 bayonets, and 8 mountain guns.

---

* Believed to have been the 2nd Battalion of the 14th Regiment; it was recalled in time for the battle of the Ya-lu, and was replaced by three battalions of Guard *Kobi* troops under Colonel Yoshida.

† All the infantry and artillery were East Siberian units. I/22nd stands for 1st Battalion, 22nd East Siberian Rifle Regiment; and 3rd/6th Battery, for 3rd Battery, 6th East Siberian Artillery Brigade.

‡ On the Ya-lu, 40 miles north-east of An-ping-ho.

§ This force was at one time under Colonel Trukhin, but the command was taken over by Colonel Kartsev some days before the battle of the Ya-lu.

‖ One squadron of this regiment was detached further up the Ya-lu with Colonel Madritov's detachment.

From Ta-tung-kou, at the mouth of the Ya-lu, to Ta-ku-shan, watching the right flank, under Major-General Mishchenko—

- 1st Chita Cossack Regiment.
- 2½ squadrons* of the 1st Verkhne-Udinsk Cossack Regiment.
- 1st Trans-Baikal Cossack Horse Battery.
- 2¾ battalions of the 21st Regiment.
- 1st/6th Battery.

In all, approximately, 1,100 sabres, 2,400 bayonets, 8 field, and 6 horse artillery guns.

In addition, the following units were in rear, guarding the line of communication, viz.—

- 2 companies of the 24th Regiment, at Feng-huang-cheng.
- 2 companies of the 24th Regiment, from Ta-ku-shan to Hai-cheng.
- 2 companies of the 24th Regiment and 1 company of the 10th Regiment, from An-tung to Lien-shan-kuan.

The combatant strength of the above troops of the Eastern Force†, excluding the seven companies on the line of communication, amounted to some 16,000 bayonets, 2,350 sabres, and 650 mounted scouts, with 48 field guns, 8 mountain guns, and 6 horse artillery guns. The extreme front watched by this force extended from Pi-tzu-wo through Ta-tung-kou to Hsiao-pu-hsi-ho, a distance of about one hundred and seventy-two miles. The line of retreat was to be on Feng-huang-cheng, but the 1st Verkhne-Udinsk Cossack Regiment was to fall back on Hai-cheng.

About this time, General Kuropatkin's dispatches to his subordinate commander on the Ya-lu are full of interest. In one he shows anxiety regarding the difficulties of retreat by the single road leading to Feng-huang-cheng, and points out the necessity for keeping it in good repair; in others he enquires whether the position at that place has been fortified, what measures have been taken to destroy supplies on retirement, and draws attention to the undesirability of any trophies falling into the hands of the Japanese. He seems to have been fully aware of General Zasulich's detailed dispositions, for he refers to the necessity of avoiding the inter-mixture of units of the two divisions, and expresses the hope that the distribution of troops, down to companies, under the command of General Kashtalinski, has been made " not contrary to the opinion of that general officer." In one of his later dispatches, received shortly before the battle, he concludes with the hope that the enemy will be resisted with the necessary firmness, but also

---

* Two and a half squadrons watched the coast line from Ta-ku-shan to Pi-tzu-wo. The 4th Squadron, as already mentioned, was at Port Arthur.

† For the order of battle of the Eastern Force, see Appendix C.

with prudence, and reminds General Zasulich that he is posted on the Ya-lu " not for a decisive action with the enemy in superior numbers." On the 25th April, he reiterates his instructions that General Zasulich's duty is to delay the crossing of the Japanese, and to observe their numbers and organization; that he is not to allow himself to be involved in an unequal combat, but should retire slowly, keeping in close touch with the enemy.*

The Japanese, on their side, had lost no time in adding to their information regarding the enemy's numbers and position. Spies, scouts, and officers with telescopes posted on the heights behind Wiju all served a useful purpose. Their task was much facilitated by the lack of concealment on the part of the Russians, who not only showed themselves on the high ground across the river but watered their horses at the Ai Ho, and exercised them on the sandy flats in the river bed. The temptation to punish them for their temerity by opening fire with artillery, although great, was resisted.

The Japanese preliminary operations.

By the 22nd April, the strength of General Zasulich's force was estimated at 5,000 cavalry, 15,000 infantry, and 60 guns, and the general line of his entrenchments and the nature of the defences about An-tung were known.†

Up to the 24th, no definite knowledge of the river had been gained, while the changes which had occurred in its channel since it was crossed in 1894, made the existing maps useless. The old fords could no longer be found, and points which had then been out of rifle range were now exposed to fire.

By the 25th, a considerable quantity of bridging material had been accumulated, but a certain amount, which had been sent round by sea, was prevented by the enemy from ascending the river to Wiju. At the same time it served to fix General Zasulich's attention on his right flank, and to deceive him as to the intended crossing higher up the stream. But the reconnaissance of the main channels of the Ai and the Ya-lu could not be completed so long as the Russian outposts held the Kyuri, Oseki, and Kintei Islands.

Capture of Kyuri, Oseki, and Kintei Islands.

On the evening of the 25th, therefore, six Japanese batteries were placed in positions whence they could shell the islands and could assist in an infantry attack. Two batteries of the Guard artillery were posted at Syohodong, two more were near Genkado, and two batteries belonging to the 12th Division were near Ryumonken. Two gunboats, two armed steamers, and two

* There is good reason to believe that General Zasulich had conflicting orders. On the one hand, General Kuropatkin intended to fight a rear-guard action; while on the other, Admiral Alexeiev pressed him to offer a vigorous resistance.

† It will be observed that the Japanese estimate of the Russian numbers only exceeded the actual force present on the 22nd April by 1,000 men. The estimate of guns was two less than the actual number.

torpedo boats from the Hosoya squadron steamed up the river to take part in the operations and, at 9.45 p.m., two battalions of the 2nd Division crossed in pontoons to Kintei Island, where they landed without opposition, and the 2nd Pioneer Battalion immediately began to throw a bridge across the river at Syohodong. This success was followed up at 4 a.m. on the 26th, when the outpost battalion of the Guards started to cross the river in pontoons and some adapted junks. All went well until mid-stream was reached, when a Russian sentry hearing the splash of oars set fire to some huts and discovered the approaching danger.* Volleys were poured upon the boats, killing and wounding several men, but the rowers kept their course and, when the shore was reached, the Russians were driven off with a loss of eighteen killed and wounded. Both Kintei and Kyuri Islands were now in Japanese hands, and these reverses led the Russians to withdraw their outposts from Tiger Hill, although they still retained possession of the village of Chukodai, which lies opposite to Wiju. There they were permitted to remain for the present, but the Japanese occupied Tiger Hill and were now able to push their outposts forward to the left bank of the main stream, as well as to send across scouting parties which interrupted communication between the Russian detachment at An-ping-ho and General Zasulich's Head-Quarters. The reconnaissance of the river could now be undertaken, and work was forthwith begun on the necessary bridges, of which ten were eventually constructed. Their aggregate length amounted to 1,630 yards,† one-third of which was built of regular pontoons, the remainder of materials obtained locally, or brought from the landing place at Rikaho.

* Some accounts state that the sentry fired torches which had been prepared.

† DETAIL OF BRIDGES CONSTRUCTED.

	Length.	Nature.	Time taken in Construction.
	Yards.		Hours.
Bridge to Kintei Island	256	Trestle	45
Bridge to Kintei Island	87	Trestle	8
Bridge A	122	Trestle	16
Bridge B	116	Trestle	13
Bridge C	37	Trestle	} 9
Bridge D	33	Trestle	
Bridge E	257	Pontoon	8
Bridge F	99	Pontoon (?)	8
Bridge G	336	Trestle	10
Bridge at Suikuchin	287	Mostly pontoon	13
Total length...	1,630	...	...

The bridging party at Syohodong was shelled by about six Russian guns posted north-east of Chiu-lien-cheng. The fire was accurate, but its effect was very slight and, as the Japanese were determined not to disclose their arrangements, they did not consider it necessary to reply, although the work of construction was considerably delayed and was not completed until the 27th. During the night of the 27th–28th, a shorter bridge was built a little lower down stream to carry guns; and between the 26th and 28th four others, A, B, C, and D, were thrown across to Kyuri Island. These last played an important part in the movement which preceded the attack, as the double means of passage which they afforded permitted wheeled traffic to come and go continuously, but the bridge at Syohodong may have been merely a blind, for no further use was made of it. All the bridges were subjected to artillery fire from time to time, but since shrapnel shell alone was fired none of them were destroyed.

Although the Russians had fallen back from Tiger Hill on the 26th, they still held the high ground to the north of it, and kept their sentries posted on the right bank of the Ya-lu. Little was known about this district but, as the plan contemplated by the Japanese involved a march across it, the Chinese inhabitants were examined and reconnaissances involving considerable risk were made by officers. From these sources it was ascertained that the ground, though difficult, was not impassable, and that it could be traversed by troops lightly equipped and also by mountain guns. Armed with this information the actual point for crossing the Ya-lu could now be fixed upon. At Suikuchin, north of Wiju, the river runs in two channels; and contrary to expectation the stream on the northern, or Russian, side was found to be the shallower. To throw a bridge to the island would not be difficult, and meanwhile a covering position could be taken upon the hills in front by troops sent across the river in pontoons. It was decided, therefore, that the 12th Division should cross at Suikuchin, and that the attack of the First Army should be delivered on a front from Chukodai to Sa-lan-kou on the Ai Ho.

Turning movement by the Japanese 12th Division.

For the proper timing of this movement, the 12th Division had to cross the Ya-lu one day before the other troops, an operation which involved its temporary isolation. It was felt, however, that the risk would not be great, for the Russians still maintained a passive attitude and did not seem to be affected by what was now proceeding on their left. Moreover, their attention had been drawn to the right by the appearance of the detachment from Admiral Hosoya's squadron on the 25th and 26th.*

At 10 a.m. on the 28th April, General Kuroki issued orders for the attack to take place on the 1st May.

General Kuroki's orders for the attack.

---

* There also appears to have been a small detachment of infantry of the 2nd Division at Yongampo, Plate I.

(1) On the 29th, the 12th Division was to cross the Ya-lu at Suikuchin and was to advance to Nan-huang-kou.

(2) On the 30th,

> The 12th Division was to advance to the line Hsia-ling-tao-kou—hill 955, and was to push out a detachment to hill 630.
>
> The 2nd Division was to assemble east of Wiju, near Shasando, by 10 p.m. and, starting at midnight, was to march by bridges C, A, E, and F to Chukodai Island*; but the artillery was to occupy its position on Kintei Island.
>
> The Guard Division was to assemble between Wiju and Hibokudo and was to follow the 2nd Division. A portion was to occupy Oseki Island, and the main body was to assemble north-east of Genkado.
>
> The howitzers were to cross to Kintei Island and were to take up positions which had been prepared.

(3) On the 1st May, the troops were to be in position at dawn,

> The 12th Division from Hsia-ling-tao-kou along the left bank of the Ai Ho to near Li-tzu-yuan. A detachment was to be sent towards Chiao-chia-kou.
>
> The 2nd Division from Hu-shan to I-ho-chien at the south end of Chukodai Island.
>
> The Guard Division from Li-tzu-yuan to Hu-shan, moving behind the 2nd Division.
>
> The reserve, which consisted of two infantry and two cavalry regiments, was to assemble on Kyuri Island and to advance to Oseki Island, with the exception of one battalion which was to act as escort to the guns on Kintei Island.

It will be observed that, in accordance with these orders, the 2nd and Guard Divisions would follow the same route. This procedure, although liable to cause delay, was necessary, because the main stream of the Ya-lu was broad and in close proximity to the enemy, and the pontoons available were only sufficient for a single bridge. The 2nd Division was to lead, for the distance to be marched by it was somewhat greater than that to be traversed by the Guards, who were not required to be in position at such an early hour as the troops on their left.

To carry out its orders and cross the Ya-lu on the night of the 29th, the 12th Division began preparations for bridging the river

---

* This island was to be reached by crossing the two bridges E and F—constructed on the 30th April—and by passing immediately north of Tiger Hill.

at an early hour on that date, and to protect the engineers engaged in the work three batteries were placed in position near Chukyuri.

The Russian troops at this point originally consisted of five companies of infantry (one battalion of the 24th Regiment and one company of the 10th Regiment), six mountain guns, and three squadrons of the Ussuri Cossack Regiment. This detachment formed part of Colonel Kartsev's flank guard and was under the command of Colonel Lechitski; but, on the morning of the 27th, that officer received orders from General Zasulich to retire to Hung-shih-la, or even to join Colonel Kartsev near Hsiao-pu-hsi-ho, if Li-tzu-yuan were occupied by the Japanese. On the morning of the 28th, Colonel Lechitski, in view of the continued presence of the Japanese on Tiger Hill and of reports that more were crossing further north, decided that the time to retire had come. He therefore withdrew with two companies of the 24th Regiment and four mountain guns to Hung-shih-la; one company of the 24th Regiment was sent to watch the roads from Hsia-ling-tao-kou, while the remainder of the detachment (two companies of infantry, two mountain guns, and three squadrons of cavalry) remained at An-ping-ho under Lieutenant-Colonel Gusev.

Movements of the Russian flank guard.

When, at 11 a.m. on the 29th, the Japanese moved forward to the river bank, covered by the fire of their batteries at Chukyuri, they encountered but little opposition, and by 2 p.m. a battalion of infantry was safely established on the right bank. In the face of greatly superior force Colonel Gusev fell back, with his infantry and guns, upon Colonel Lechitski at Hung-shih-la, and at the same time sent his cavalry to join the remainder of the left flank detachment under Colonel Kartsev. As soon as General Zasulich received news of the activity of the 12th Japanese Division he decided to send a battalion of the 22nd Regiment and four guns of the 3rd/6th Battery to join Colonel Lechitski. This reinforcement would, it was hoped, be sufficient to force the Japanese back across the Ya-lu, for the movement of the 12th Division was still regarded as a mere feint. This view of the situation was apparently shared at the army Head-Quarters, for when a report of what had occurred was sent to General Kuropatkin, he replied that the detachment at An-ping-ho seemed to have fallen back too hastily and too far, and that it was important not to lose touch of the enemy. According to his view the Japanese operations against General Zasulich's left were wanting in that energy which usually betokens a movement more serious than a mere demonstration. Nevertheless, he impressed upon his subordinate the necessity for keeping a careful watch along the whole front of his position, and for preparing for a serious attack upon his left and centre, a counsel which was reiterated in a later despatch. However, the order to reinforce Colonel Lechitski appears to have been delayed, for it was not at once carried into effect, and on the 30th it was countermanded.

The crossing of the Ya-lu, the 29th April.

Meanwhile the passage of the river by the leading troops of the 12th Japanese Division had been immediately followed by the construction of a bridge across the main stream of the Ya-lu. At the site selected the river was two hundred and twenty yards wide, twenty-four feet deep, and flowed with a velocity of about four miles an hour. Numerous anchors were required to keep the pontoons in position, and, as military material was not forthcoming in sufficient quantities, some native junks were used.

On this date, the 29th, while the rest of the First Army was waiting for the 12th Division to establish itself on the right bank, a small force of Russians suddenly assumed the offensive further south. At 4 p.m., a battalion of the 22nd East Siberian Rifle Regiment, the mounted scouts of the 10th and 12th Regiments, and two guns of the 3rd/6th Battery, crossed the valley of the Ai from opposite Li-tzu-yuan, and supported by artillery fire from Po-te-tien-tzu, forced the Guards' outpost company on Tiger Hill to fall back to Kyuri Island. The retreat was conducted in good order, and, as the enemy did not show himself over the brow of the hill, only a few shells were fired by the Guard Artillery. The loss of the hill in no way affected General Kuroki's plans, but prevented bridge E from being made during the night of the 29th, as had been intended, and to facilitate its rapid construction on the following day, materials were collected near Genkado.

The same night, with the view to assisting the 12th Division to occupy its allotted position on the right of the army, the artillery of the 2nd Division and the howitzers crossed the short bridge leading to Kintei, and were entrenched before daybreak in the sandy soil of that island. In order effectually to conceal the howitzers, screens of drift timber and trees were placed a short distance in front of the batteries; great care was also exercised lest the general view of the landscape should appear altered from the Russian side. Water was thrown in front of the batteries to keep down dust, platforms were erected, hidden in trees on the flanks, whence officers could watch the fire effect, and two observation posts connected with the batteries by telephone were placed upon the hills south of Wiju. These posts and the batteries were furnished with duplicate maps of the enemy's position, divided into squares, so that observers might direct the fire of the howitzers on any point where a suitable target appeared. So well were the howitzers hidden, that on this date and on the 1st May not a single Russian shell reached them. As a further precaution both the howitzers and the guns of the 2nd Division were to remain silent on the 30th April. Their orders, however, allowed them to fire if a good opportunity arose, or to reply if the enemy opened a cannonade.

On the morning of the 30th April, the Russians who had occupied Tiger Hill on the previous evening were observed to be busily engaged in entrenching themselves, whereupon the artillery of the Guard Division opened fire. No reply came from the enemy's guns, whose custom it had been to

The 30th April.

shell the Japanese daily about 7 a.m. At 10 a.m., some Japanese engineers in two or three boats began the survey of the main stream opposite Chukodai, and at 10.30 a.m. the 2nd/6th Battery, posted on the high ground north-east of Chiu-lien-cheng, opened fire upon them. The guns and howitzers on Kintei Island replied, and in half-an-hour the Russian artillery was silenced.* About 11 a.m., four guns from the 3rd/6th Battery opened fire from the knoll east of Ma-kou, but were silenced by a few rounds from three batteries of the Guard Artillery, which had advanced to Kyuri Island at 4 a.m.

While this artillery duel was in progress* the 12th Division was approaching its allotted position. The bridge at Suikuchin was to have been ready at midnight, but unexpected difficulties delayed its completion until 3 a.m. on the 30th. At that hour the division began to cross in three detachments; and at 6.20 a.m. the leading troops, the 14th and 46th Regiments and a battery of artillery, under Major-General Kigoshi reached the further bank. One company was left in An-ping-ho, and the remaining troops were divided into two columns. The right column marched south-west towards the Hu Shan ridge, where it arrived soon after 11 a.m., while the left column marched down the river bank. About noon the hill 955 was reached and a party was at once pushed out to the height 630. Immediately behind General Kigoshi's brigade, General Sasaki crossed the bridge, and forded the western branch of the river with the 47th Regiment, a squadron of cavalry, and a battery of artillery, and at 5.30 p.m. he occupied the high ground east of Hsia-ling-tao-kou. By 1 p.m. the remainder of the division reached Nan-huang-kou, where a halt of some hours was made before moving up in line with the other troops.

As the advance of the 46th Regiment threatened their retreat, the Russians on Tiger Hill retired about midday, and the covering party of the Guards immediately retook possession of the hill, where they came into touch with the left of the 12th Division. The Japanese movement was also reported to Major-General Kashtalinski, who had replaced General Trusov† in command of the troops at Chiu-lien-cheng That officer forthwith despatched half of the 1/22nd Regiment to Ching-kou, to join the other half of the same battalion and the two guns of the 3rd/6th Battery, which had been posted there on the 28th to guard the left flank. At the same time he reported the situation to General Zasulich, who informed him in reply that the 2nd Battalion of the 11th Regiment was on its way to join him from Tien-tzu, and that he was to maintain his position.

The retreat of the Russians was the signal for work to begin on the bridges at E, F, and G, and by 8 p.m. all except the last were ready. During the day arrangements were made to transport

* The casualties in the 2nd/6th Battery during the bombardment were 5 officers and 26 men killed and wounded.

† General Trusov had fallen sick on the 28th.

the artillery of the 2nd Division across the main stream of the Ya-lu, in order that it might support the attack of the infantry of that division at a range closer than was possible from its position on Kintei Island. To bridge the stream, which opposite the batteries was five hundred yards in width, was impossible, and it was decided therefore to send the guns across at night on pontoon ferries, of which twenty-one were constructed behind Genkado and floated down to Kintei Island. Such was the difficulty of the operation, due to the necessity of working in the dark, that by daybreak on the 1st May only three batteries and the battalion of infantry forming the escort had crossed and entrenched themselves.

At 8 p.m. on the 30th April, the 2nd Division moved off from Shasando,* and by 10.30 p.m. had reached Oseki village, leaving the bridges clear for the Guard Division which was following. At 2.30 a.m., the 2nd Division again moved forward and crossed the bridge to Tiger Hill, after which Chukodai Island was reached by fording one of the channels of the Ai. By daybreak on the 1st May this division was entrenched in the open within two thousand yards of the Russian position, the batteries which had been ferried across the main stream being posted on its left immediately north of Chukodai village. Further north, the Guards, whose march had been delayed by the necessity of using the same bridge as the 2nd Division, reached their allotted ground about 5 a.m. and likewise entrenched themselves; while on their right stood the 12th Division, which had also moved down from the high ground to the left bank of the Ai Ho. Three days' supplies for the whole army had been collected, and on the 30th April the base at Rikaho was closed, the boats there being ordered to proceed to the south of An-tung, where they would await the issue of the battle.

The 1st May.

The blow which had been preceded by such elaborate and deliberate preparations, was now about to fall. Frequent warnings from the Russian commander-in-chief and reports from General Kashtalinski had not availed to impress General Zasulich with the danger on his left, and he still seems to have clung to the belief that the Japanese would land an army on his right. But for this he was not altogether to blame. Colonel Kartsev with a considerable force of cavalry had been posted on the upper Ya-lu for the express purpose of watching the movements of the Japanese right. But during the 30th, instead of keeping in touch with the enemy, he not only fell back from the river without attempting to harass the enemy's advance, but also failed to inform his superiors of the action which he had taken. Moreover the naval feints near the mouth of the Ya-lu, which were repeated on the 29th and 30th April, and the appearance of vessels in the offing, served their purpose, and the main portion of the Eastern Force still remained massed at Tien-tzu and An-tung, while three Japanese divisions were quietly concentrating against the opposite flank.

* The 2nd Division had been ordered originally to march at midnight (see p. 62), an hour which must have been altered subsequently to 8 p.m.

The battle was to be fought on a front from Chiu-lien-cheng to Ching-kou and here General Kashtalinski, who had been ordered to maintain his ground had, on the 30th, disposed his troops as follows*:—

Distribution of the Russian troops.

Right Section. From Chiu-lien-cheng to Yao-kou, under Colonel Tsibulski.

> 1st, 2nd, and 3rd Battalions of the 12th Regiment.
> 3 companies of the 2nd Battalion of the 11th Regiment.
> 1 company of the 2nd Battalion of the 24th Regiment.†
> 2nd Battery of the 6th Artillery Brigade.

Left Section. From Ma-kou through Po-te-tien-tzu to Ching-kou, under Colonel Gromov.

> 1st, 2nd, and 3rd Battalions of the 22nd Regiment.
> 1 company of the 2nd Battalion of the 11th Regiment.
> 3rd Battery of the 6th Artillery Brigade.

Thus a force of little more than seven battalions and sixteen guns was distributed over a front of some six miles, and was about to bear the whole brunt of the Japanese attack. Both the batteries had been subjected to Japanese artillery fire, and the 2nd/6th Battery, which had lost several officers, had withdrawn on the night of the 30th to a position about one mile west

---

* See Map I/2.
The troops of the left section were distributed as follows:—
  (a) On the high ground north-east of Ma-kou—
    10th and 11th Companies of the 22nd Regiment.
  (b) In rear of (a)—
    3rd/6th Battery (6 guns only; 2 guns of this battery had been detached to Ching-kou with the I/22nd Regiment).
  (c) North of Po-te-tien-tzu—
    7th Company of the 11th Regiment, and 12th Company of the 22nd Regiment.
  d) Further up the Ai Ho, separated from the rest of the force south of it by a gap nearly 2,000 yards wide—
    5th Company of the 22nd Regiment.
  (e) Sectional reserve, behind the right flank—
    6th, 7th, 8th, and 9th Companies of the 22nd Regiment.

The troops of the right section were as follows:—
  (a) On the right, south-west of Chui-lien-cheng—
    5th, 6th, and 8th Companies of the 11th Regiment, and 8th Company, 24th Regiment.
  (b) North of Chiu-lien-cheng—
    2nd, 3rd, 4th, 6th, 9th, and 12th Companies of the 12th Regiment.
  (c) In rear of (b) as local reserve—
    7th and 8th Companies of the 12th Regiment.
  (d) Sectional reserve—
    1st, 5th, 10th, and 11th Companies of the 12th Regiment and the machine gun company.
  (e) About a mile west of Chiu-lien-cheng—
    2nd/6th Battery.

† This company had been called up from the line of communication in order to take part in the battle.

of Chiu-lien-cheng. Moreover, the bombardment had not been without effect upon the infantry, and at 11 p.m. on that date Colonel Tsibulski, who commanded the 12th Regiment, pointed out to General Kashtalinski that the shells of the Japanese guns of position were quite " unbearable, and that he could not guarantee the quiet withdrawal of his men from their trenches if fire were specially directed upon them, on the following day."* He added that the Japanese were undoubtedly in superior force, and that there was every reason to expect an assault. Upon this General Kashtalinski dispatched a telegram to General Zasulich at San-cheng-kou, in which, after a brief description of the bombardment, he suggested that his force should occupy the heights behind Chiu-lien-cheng during the night, leaving outposts in the advanced trenches with orders to fall back at daylight. General Zasulich replied that the troops were at no point to evacuate the ground occupied, but that he had decided that in the event of a bombardment, they were to leave outposts on the original positions and to withdraw to the nearest heights with a view to taking cover, but not of retiring. At 3 a.m. on the 1st May, a report came in from the 12th Regiment that the sound of wheels on the islands and of guns crossing bridges was audible, and it became evident that the Japanese were preparing to attack. No change was, however, made in the strength of the groups at An-tung and Tien-tzu, except that the machine gun company was sent to General Kashtalinski.

When day broke a thick fog hung over the valley between the opposing armies, but about 6 a.m. it began to lift, and the Japanese howitzers opened fire. At first no reply came from the Russian side, and for a brief space it seemed to the Japanese as if the enemy had fallen back. Suddenly the six guns near Ma-kou replied, but in a few minutes they were silenced, and the whole of the Japanese artillery was turned against the shelter trenches of the infantry.

The attack of the Japanese had originally been planned to begin with the turning movement of the 12th Division on their right, where the least resistance was expected, and as soon as its advance had sufficiently developed the Guard and 2nd Divisions were to move. But, about 7 a.m., as the Russians brought no other artillery into action after the battery near Ma-kou had been silenced, General Kuroki, who had taken up his position near Genkado, ordered a simultaneous advance of all three divisions.

At the word of command the Japanese rose from their trenches and surged across the space between them and the enemy, their dark blue uniforms rendering them conspicuous objects on the yellow sandy plain. No shot greeted their thick line of skirmishers until the Ai Ho was reached, when the Russians opened

The Japanese advance to the attack.

---

* According to a Russian authority, the 12th Regiment had suffered, on the 30th April, a loss of 3 officers and 20 rank and file killed and wounded.

a heavy fire of volleys at distances varying from 1,500 to 1,200 paces. To cross a swiftly-flowing river whose waters run breast-high is, under no conditions, a very simple matter, but the same operation performed under a hail of bullets by troops burdened with arms and ammunition* makes the preservation of order extremely difficult. Thus by the time that the Japanese had arrived in mid-stream their formations were disorganized, and the men, crowded together in places, were suffering many losses, some of the wounded being drowned. Nevertheless the advance was steadily pursued, and on reaching the further bank individual fire was opened. During the infantry advance the divisional artillery had ceaselessly shelled the Russian infantry position, while the howitzers, still using indirect fire, searched the ground in rear of it.

While crossing the river, the 2nd Division, whose attack brought it opposite the right section of the Russian position from Chiu-lien-cheng to Yao-kou, suffered considerable loss, more especially on its left, which for a time was held in check. But the 4th and 29th Regiments which formed the right were able to push on and succeeded in forcing the Russians to leave their trenches, and fall back to a second position on the hills in rear, exposing themselves as they did so to the fire of the Japanese artillery. The 6th Company of the 12th East Siberian Rifle Regiment tried to cover the retreat by a bayonet charge, but the Japanese skirmishers, giving way before it, cleared the front of their reserves, whose fire drove it off. The advance was then continued, and the safety of the Russian battery, which though out of action had remained in position, became endangered.

<small>2nd Division.</small>

While the right of the 2nd Division was progressing, the left began again to move forward and threatened to surround Colonel Tsibulski's force. This danger was observed by General Kashtalinski, whose left section, under Colonel Gromov, was already falling back. About 8.30 a.m., therefore, he ordered Colonel Tsibulski to withdraw his troops to a position† behind the Han-tu-ho-tzu stream, where he hoped to be able to delay the Japanese advance against his right. This position had been previously selected and General Zasulich himself, after conferring with General Kashtalinski, had decided that the time to occupy it had arrived. The operation of withdrawal was difficult, for the right of the Japanese 2nd Division had made considerable progress, but was covered by the fire of the 2nd/6th Battery and by the machine gun company.

---

* The 12th Division carried lightened knapsacks. The Guard and 2nd Divisions carried spare ammunition and rations in the blue cloth holdall worn *en bandoulière*, but discarded their knapsacks before the attack.

† This position, which is several times referred to in the narrative, was situated on the high ground immediately west of the words Han-tu-ho-tzu R. on Map I/2.

On the right of the 2nd Division the advance of the Guard Division brought it opposite the left section of the Russian line of defence, whose baggage had been sent back to Ching-kou. The 3rd/6th Battery, which had reserved its fire for the infantry attack, was silenced by the Japanese artillery, and the right of the Guard Division soon penetrated between Po-te-tien-tzu and the 5th Company of the 22nd Regiment, imperilling the position of the troops further south, who were fully engaged with those immediately in front of them. To restore the situation by bringing up fresh troops was impossible, for the sectional reserve was too far distant and its help was urgently required on the right.

The Guard Division.

At this juncture, a report was received that the Japanese were coming on in force against the left flank. Thereupon Colonel Gromov rode in that direction and saw some five or six hostile battalions advancing from the heights on the left bank of the Ai Ho, about one mile north-east of his position. It appeared evident to him that the enemy's main attack was directed against Po-te-tien-tzu, and that the 5th Company of the 22nd Regiment could not prevent the threatening movement. About 8.30 a.m., therefore, he decided to recall that company, throw back his left and take up a position on the ridge which runs parallel to the Ching-kou road, where he hoped to be joined by the I/22nd Regiment and the two guns of the 3rd/6th Battery. Orders were sent to the sectional reserve to occupy the ridge and cover the retirement of the fighting line, the left of which would fall back first. Scarcely had these orders been dispatched when the commander of the 3rd/6th Battery reported that the right of Colonel Gromov's section of defence was turned and that his guns could no longer remain in their present position. The inner flanks of the Guard and 2nd Divisions had both broken through the Russian front between Yao-kou and Ma-kou, and the battery was in imminent danger of capture. It was therefore ordered to fall back, and the 7th Company of the 22nd Regiment, from the sectional reserve, was detailed to act as escort. The three remaining companies of the sectional reserve began, about 9 a.m., to withdraw to the ridge in rear, being followed by the 5th and 12th Companies of the 22nd Regiment, which had formed the left of the firing line.

Meantime the 3rd/6th Battery, accompanied by its escort and by the 10th Company of the 22nd Regiment which had originally been posted in front of it, had begun to retire; but so steep was the ground over which it had to move that the guns had to be unlimbered and man-handled one by one down the western slope of the

Retirement of Colonel Gromov.

---

* Major-General Kashtalinski had directed Colonel Gromov, in the event of serious action, to send his transport to Ching-kou, whence he was to retire by Liu-chia-kou. From the latter place Feng-huang-cheng can be reached by a road which is practically parallel to the An-tung–Feng-huang-cheng highway.

abandoned position, an operation which was carried out under heavy rifle fire from the Japanese on the left bank of the Ai Ho. When, shortly after 9 a.m., the battery reached the lower ground it must have found the road leading northward to be impassable or already commanded by the enemy's fire, for instead of making for Ching-kou it proceeded in a southerly direction towards Chiu-lien-cheng. This movement was observed by Colonel Gromov, who directed it to turn about in the direction of Po-te-tien-tzu and thence to move on Ching-kou. The battery now seems to have outstripped its escort, whose strength had been augmented by the 7th Company of the 11th Regiment and the 11th Company of the 22nd Regiment, which had joined it on the march. On reaching Po-te-tien-tzu the commander found the road to Ching-kou blocked by the enemy and decided to retire by Chiu-lien-cheng. The guns were once more turned about and proceeded towards Ma-kou, near which place they were captured by the 3rd Regiment of the Japanese Guard Division.

In the meantime, Colonel Gromov, after dispatching orders to the battery, had grown anxious lest his own line of retreat should be intercepted by the advancing Japanese, and had decided not to hold a second position, but to retire with his five remaining companies to Ching-kou.* The Russian detachment at that place faced the right wing of the 12th Division, whose advance was slow, for the men were much fatigued by their exertions since crossing the Ya-lu on the night of the 29th April. Moreover, the left battalions of the division had to cross the Ai Ho at a point where the water was deep, and, though no enemy opposed them, the heights at Fang-tai-tung-tzu were not reached till nearly 9 a.m.

When the 1st Battalion of the 14th Regiment and the mountain battery which formed the extreme right of General Kuroki's army reached Tuan-shan-tzu, the I/22nd Regiment and the two guns of the 3rd/6th Battery finding their flank threatened began to retire. This movement was perceived by Colonel Gromov, who, while falling back with the 2nd and 3rd Battalions† of that regiment, had observed some six or seven Japanese battalions pushing forward over the heights north of Po-te-tien-tzu. No sooner did the two Russian guns come into view, crossing the hill south of Ching-kou in the direction of Lao-fang-kou, than he decided to incline westward and to take up a position on the saddle over which runs the road between those two places.

* The 5th, 6th, 8th, 9th, and 12th Companies of the 22nd Regiment. The 7th and 10th Companies, after becoming separated from the guns, joined Colonel Gromov on the march, while the 7th Company of the 11th Regiment and the 11th Company of the 22nd Regiment turned westward across the hills. The 7th Company, 11th Regiment, made its way to Tien-tzu, and the 11th Company, 22nd Regiment, took part in fighting which occurred later in the day near Ha-ma-tang.

† The 11th Company of the 3rd Battalion was not present, having fallen back independently after accompanying the 3rd/6th Battery when it first retreated towards Chiu-lien-cheng.

The general situation at this period as regards the Russians was as follows: In the original disposition seven battalions and sixteen guns had held the front from Chiu-lien-cheng to Ching-kou. Of this force the greater portion of the right section and the detachment at Ching-kou had succeeded in retiring in fair order, while of the remainder, which was under Colonel Gromov's command, six guns had been captured and two battalions, greatly shaken, had fallen back. To delay the enemy's further advance, General Kashtalinksi had at hand the 12th Regiment, the 5th, 6th, and 8th Companies of the 11th Regiment, the 8th Company of the 24th Regiment, the 2nd/6th Battery, and the machine gun company. All of these troops had been engaged, and with them he now proceeded to take position on the right bank of the Han-tu-ho-tzu stream.*

Situation of Russians about 9 a.m.

On the right at An-tung nothing had occurred beyond the appearance in the river of a Japanese flotilla which had shelled the Russian position on that flank and had engaged the attention of the artillery. The three battalions posted near An-tung, and the reserve of five battalions and eight guns at Tien-tzu, had remained inactive and had taken no share in the battle on their left.

On the Japanese side, the 2nd Division was concentrating in the neighbourhood of Chiu-lien-cheng with the general reserve, which had advanced at 8 a.m., on its right at Suribachi Yama; the Guards were on the hills between Yao-kou and Po-te-tien-tzu; the left wing of the 12th Division was on the hill north of Po-te-tien-tzu, and the right was climbing the ridge west of Fang-tai-tung-tzu. The artillery was placed as follows: Two batteries of the 2nd Division had forded the river opposite Chiu-lien-cheng and were close to that place; the remaining batteries of the division were in position at the southern extremity of the island of Chukodai. The Guard Artillery had crossed the branch of the Ai Ho near Tiger Hill by an improvised bridge, and had taken position between Yao-kou and Ma-kou; the 12th Artillery Regiment had also crossed to the right bank of the Ai Ho, and the howitzers remained on Kintei Island.

Situation of the Japanese about 9 a.m.

The Japanese had captured the Russian first position about 9 a.m., and General Kuroki then decided to advance to the line of the Ha-ma-tang River, and with this object fresh orders were at once issued. The reserve, which was now christened the "Pursuing Detachment," was to advance along the main Feng-huang-cheng road.

Second phase of the battle.

---

* The withdrawal to the position on the Han-tu-ho-tzu stream was covered by the 5th and 6th Companies of the 11th Regiment and the 8th Company of the 24th Regiment. After carrying out the duty assigned to them these companies fell back to Tien-tzu. The 8th Company of the 11th Regiment remained with the 12th Regiment.

The Guards were to occupy the hills about Ha-ma-tang. The 2nd Division was to move to An-tung; and the 12th Division was to march south to Ta-lou-fang, sending a detachment towards Liu-chia-kou. The 12th Division had already anticipated these orders and, after driving off the Russian detachment at Ching-kou, immediately pushed southward along the road to Ha-ma-tang. The Guard and 2nd Divisions were, however, stubbornly opposed by General Kashtalinski in his new position behind the Han-tu-ho-tzu and found that they could not advance until the artillery could be brought up to their support. This delay was just sufficient to enable General Zasulich to draw in the troops on his right flank. At 9.35 a.m., the commander at An-tung had been directed to withdraw immediately to Tien-tzu, after burning the supplies collected at the former place. When the order reached him his force was somewhat scattered, the 2nd Company of the 10th Regiment and two guns of the 1st/3rd Battery being at San-chia-kou, some five miles to the south-west; while posted on the flanks and on the island of Kanshi were the mounted scouts of the 10th and 24th Infantry Regiments. Orders were sent to the detachment at San-chia-kou to retire direct to Tang-shan-cheng on the road to Feng-huang-cheng, and by noon the troops at An-tung were falling back to Tien-tzu. To cover this retirement the two battalions of the 11th East Siberian Rifle Regiment and the battery were sent from Tien-tzu to join General Kashtalinski on the Han-tu-ho-tzu stream, and that officer was told that he must resist the Japanese advance until the troops on his right had made good their retreat. For the next two hours the position in the centre remained unchanged, for the Japanese were awaiting the arrival of their artillery, but to the north the position of the Russian troops was more difficult, for the 12th Japanese Division was advancing as quickly as circumstances would permit, and of this danger General Kashtalinski was still ignorant.

About 11 a.m., the 1st Battalion of the 14th Japanese Regiment and six guns issued from the village of Ching-kou, but their further advance was checked by Colonel Gromov, who was posted north of Ta-lou-fang and was joined almost at the same moment by the 1st Battalion of the 22nd Regiment. More Japanese troops could now be seen on the right bank of the river, and Colonel Gromov decided to make good his retreat, while there was yet time, through Lao-fang-kou and Liu-chia-kou. He first sent off his wounded, then the two guns and the 2nd, 3rd, 7th, and 10th Companies and was preparing to follow with the rest of his command, when, about 1 p.m., an officer of General Zasulich's staff rode up and ordered him to retreat by Lao-chou-tun. Colonel Gromov now marched the remnant of his force to that place, passing through it about 1.30 p.m., and reaching the line of communication without further loss.*

* As the eleven companies with Colonel Gromov all reached the Feng-huang-cheng road through Lao-chou-tun, it would seem that the four leading companies were recalled from the direction of Liu-chia-kou.

As soon as he had brought his troops through Ching-kou, General Kigoshi ordered the 24th Regiment to advance on Ha-ma-tang and to occupy the hills north-east of that village. Hoping to cut off the main body of the enemy from their line of retreat on Feng-huang-cheng, the colonel of the 24th Regiment told off one battalion to advance at once, leaving his other two battalions to reform after their fight and to come on as quickly as possible. One battalion of the 46th was to follow the 24th. At 12.30 p.m., as the leading Japanese troops arrived within a mile of Ta-lou-fang, two bodies of Russians were seen to be retiring covered by a rear guard. These were Colonel Gromov's troops, and it was not until 1.40 p.m. when the battalion of the 46th Regiment had come up on the right of the 24th and the Russian rear guard had retired, that the advance could be resumed. Then, at 2 p.m., another body of about a thousand Russians appeared on the hills north-east of Ha-ma-tang, and the 12th Division was again checked. These fresh troops were the reinforcements for General Kashtalinski, who had evacuated his second position and was now retiring on Ha-ma-tang. Between 11 a.m. and noon, while General Kashtalinski was waiting for the two battalions of the 11th Regiment to arrive, an assistant-surgeon of the 6th East Siberian Rifle Division had reported to him that the 22nd Regiment on the extreme left was routed, and that the Japanese had occupied Liu-chia-kou. Up to this moment no anxiety had been felt regarding that flank, for no reports had been received from Colonel Gromov,* who was believed still to be holding Ching-kou. General Kashtalinski at once dispatched towards that place the mounted scouts of the 12th Regiment, who shortly afterwards reported that a Japanese column, in strength about a regiment of infantry, was moving from Ching-kou on Lao-fang-kou, and that a force of cavalry was also visible in the same direction. General Kashtalinski then rode out himself, and finding that his left was seriously threatened, sent orders to Lieutenant-Colonel Linda, his chief staff officer, who was with the troops on the right bank of the Han-tu-ho-tzu, to retire at once to Tien-tzu. At this moment the 11th Company of the 22nd Regiment, which had been with Colonel Gromov's guns, happened to come up and was posted on some high ground facing north, whence it was ordered to delay the enemy's advance; and about the same time orders were sent to the two battalions of the 11th East Siberian Rifle Regiment, which were coming from the reserve to occupy the height 570. These two battalions had already passed through a difficult defile just east of Ha-ma-tang, but as soon as they were met by their fresh orders they turned northward and took up the required position. The battery, which was following the infantry, was, at the same time, ordered to return through Ha-ma-

---

* Colonel Gromov dispatched a report at 12.15 p.m., in which he stated that he was retiring, but it was not received by General Kashtalinski until about 4 p.m.

tang to the Feng-huang-cheng road, for the ground was difficult even for the movement of infantry, and it was felt that the guns would hamper rather than assist the retreat.

A little after 2 p.m., as its eight wagons reached the northern mouth of the gorge, about 1,000 yards south-east of Ha-ma-tang, they came under fire from the 5th Company of the 24th Japanese Regiment, which had outstripped the other units of the 12th Division and had reached the north-west slopes of the group of hills that overlook the road. The movement was continued at a trot, and the wagons made their way in safety to Tien-tzu, but the guns, which were following, soon lost several horses and, as it seemed impossible to retire under the enemy's fire, the commander decided to bring them into action in support of the two battalions of the 11th Regiment, which were engaged with the 24th Japanese Regiment, and were covering the defile through which General Kashtalinski must retire.

When Lieutenant-Colonel Linda received General Kashtalinski's order to retire to Tien-tzu, he moved his troops off in the following order : first the companies of the 12th Regiment which had been in reserve, next the machine gun company and the 2nd/6th Battery, escorted by the 8th Company of the 11th Regiment, then the remainder of the 12th Regiment, of which the 5th Company formed the rear guard. As they approached the defile they were fired upon, and the machine gun company, without waiting for orders, took post on the southern slopes to cover the entrance from that side. General Kashtalinski also detached two companies from his column to strengthen his rear guard, and these were followed shortly afterwards by three more companies. In this way the column gained the defile and was just debouching from the northern end when the 12th Regiment came under long range fire from the north-east of Ha-ma-tang. The scouts advanced towards the enemy, and covered by their fire the regiment was able to continue its march to the Feng-huang-cheng road. The 2nd/6th Battery, which was following the infantry, on passing the south-eastern slopes of height 570 where part of the 3rd/3rd Battery was already in position, found itself exposed to a heavy rifle fire from the north and halted under cover of a slope. Lieutenant-Colonel Linda then came up, and, recognizing the impossibility of continuing the movement by the road, decided to withdraw by a circuitous route leaving height 570 in a southerly direction. The battery moved off but after covering about two thousand yards found the ground too steep for further movement, and returned to join the 3rd/3rd Battery.

The fighting soon became very severe, particularly on the left of the 24th Japanese Regiment where the 5th Company was losing heavily. This company had pushed forward with great gallantry in front of the remainder of its battalion and might have been annihilated but for the timely arrival of three batteries of the 12th Division and of the leading troops of the Guard and 2nd Divisions.

As already explained the movements of these two divisions had been delayed by the difficulty of transporting the guns across the Ai Ho, but when the Russians began to evacuate the position on the Han-tu-ho-tzu stream General Kuroki, who was now at Suribachi Yama, at once gave orders for the advance to be resumed.

About 2 p.m., the Guards and the "Pursuing Detachment" moved across the Han-tu-ho-tzu. Two hours later they drove the Russian rear guard out of Chuan-shan-tzu, and forced it to abandon four guns, which had been swung round to face the attack from the east;

Surrender of the Russian rear guard.

but for some time longer they could not take possession of their prize and the guns remained derelict between the combatants. Seeing that the resistance was weakening the 12th Division supported by the guns, now made a determined attack upon the 11th East Siberian Rifle Regiment and drove it off the hills north of Ha-ma-tang. The 2nd Guard Brigade and the "Pursuing Detachment" then advanced against the six or seven hundred men who were still holding out on the high ground south-east of the village, about point 420, and soon after 5 p.m. drove them down into the arms of the 46th and 24th Regiments. There the remnant of the rear guard was at last forced to surrender, and eleven field guns and seven machine guns fell into the hands of the Japanese.

This disaster to the Russian arms may partly be attributed to Colonel Gromov's failure to keep General Kashtalinski informed of his movements* and of the advance of the Japanese 12th Division. At the same time it must not be forgotten that by its gallant action the Russian rear guard had performed its allotted task. For while it held the hills round Ha-ma-tang the main body was falling back towards Feng-huang-cheng covered by the 10th Regiment and the two guns of the 3rd/6th Battery from Ching-kou.

At Tien-tzu the wagons of the 3rd/3rd Battery and portions of the 11th, 12th, and 22nd Regiments succeeded in joining the retreating column, and soon after nightfall Tang-shan-cheng, a post on the line of communication, was reached. On the

Concentration of the Russian force at Feng-huang-cheng.

following day the whole force was concentrated at Feng-huang-cheng, with the exception of the 9th and 10th Regiments and the batteries which were left at Pien-mien to check the pursuit; but beyond sending out a few cavalry patrols the Japanese made no attempt to follow up their victory.

The losses in officers and men suffered by the Russians† in the battle of the 1st of May are not accurately known, but some fourteen hundred dead were buried by the Japanese, and about six hundred prisoners, many of whom were wounded, were taken. In addition to these, some wounded were carried from the field by the Russians, whose total casualties

Losses.

---

* Colonel Gromov was tried by court martial and eventually shot himself.
† For losses of the Japanese and Russians, see Appendix C.

probably amounted to not less than three thousand of all ranks, or about three times those of the Japanese. Of the twenty-four guns of the three Russian batteries which were engaged, twenty-one fell into the hands of the Japanese, while eight machine guns and nineteen ammunition wagons were included among the spoils of war.

APPENDIX A.

STRENGTH OF THE RUSSIAN TROOPS IN THE FAR EAST, *i.e.*, EAST OF LAKE BAIKAL, AT THE BEGINNING OF FEBRUARY, 1904.

(*See* Strategical Map I.)

The troops in these tables have been classified as follows:—

Field Troops.—Troops which form the first line available for field operations.

Fortress Troops.—Troops specially organized for service in the fortress to which they are allotted.

Railway Troops.—Troops employed in the construction of the railway line.

Frontier Guards.—The special force of all arms whose primary duty was to guard the railway, but which was also available for service in the field.

A.—*Field Troops.*

Although the established war strength of a battalion of infantry and a squadron is about 1,000 rifles and 155 sabres, at no period of the war were these units up to their full numbers. If the average combatant strength of an infantry battalion be taken at 700, and that of a squadron at 120, the field troops may be summarized as follows:—

Infantry.	Battalions.	Estimated Strength.
1st, 2nd, 3rd, 4th, 5th and 6th East Siberian Rifle Brigades	48	33,600
7th* East Siberian Rifle Brigade	12	8,400
8th* East Siberian Rifle Brigade	8	5,600
9th† East Siberian Rifle Brigade	12	8,400
2nd Brigade,‡ 31st Infantry Division (Xth Army Corps)	8	5,600
2nd Brigade,‡ 35th Infantry Division (XVIIth Army Corps)	8	5,600
1st§ Siberian (Reserve) Infantry Brigade	4	2,800
Total Infantry	100	70,000

* These Brigades had been recently formed from the fortress infantry regiments of Port Arthur and Vladivostok respectively. They were intended for the mobile defence of the fortresses of Port Arthur and Vladivostok, but were not to form part of the field armies.

† The formation of this brigade was carried out, during the period of mobilization, by means of drafts from European Russia. The four regiments composing this brigade were not completed before the 18th February.

‡ These brigades, with part of their artillery, were moved to the Far East during the latter half of 1903.

§ This brigade (consisting of the 1st Strietensk, 2nd Chita, 3rd Nerchinsk and 4th Verkhne-Udinsk battalions) would, on mobilization, expand into a division of 16 battalions, having an estimated strength of 14,000 men. In view of the large number of reservists required to complete the war establishment, it is probable that this brigade did not complete its mobilization and expansion until considerably later. This view is confirmed by the fact that the division formed by this brigade was at Harbin at the end of April, and only reached Mukden in May, notwithstanding the urgent need for troops at the front.

Cavalry.	Squadrons.	Estimated Strength.
Primorsk Dragoon Regiment	6	720
1st Nerchinsk Trans-Baikal Cossack Regiment	6	720
1st Chita Trans-Baikal Cossack Regiment	6	720
1st Argun Trans-Baikal Cossack Regiment	6	720
1st Verkhne-Udinsk Trans-Baikal Cossack Regiment	6	720
Amur Cossack Division	3	360
Ussuri Cossack Division*	2	240
Total Cavalry	35	4,200

* These squadrons expanded into six squadrons on mobilization. It is not known to what extent this expansion was completed in the early days of February.

Artillery.	Batteries.	Estimated Strength.	Guns.
1st East Siberian Artillery Brigade	8*	2,120	64
2nd East Siberian Artillery Brigade	4	984	32
Trans-Baikal Cossack Horse Artillery	2	476	12
East Siberian Rifle Artillery Division	3	783	24
Trans-Baikal Artillery Division	2	521	16
31st Artillery Brigade	3	783	24
35th Artillery Brigade	3	783	24
Total Artillery	25	6,450	196

* Two of these were mountain batteries.

Engineers.	Companies.	Estimated Strength.
1st and 2nd East Siberian Sapper Battalions	8	1,612
3rd East Siberian Sapper Battalion*	4	808
Kuan-tung Sapper Company	1	280
Total Engineers	13	2,700

* Formed on 14th February.

Summary of Field Troops.	Estimated Strength.
Infantry.—100 Battalions	70,000 rifles, with 8 machine guns.
Cavalry.—35 Squadrons	4,200 sabres.
Artillery.—25 Batteries	6,450 men, with 196 guns.
Engineers.—13 Companies	2,700
Total Field Troops	83,350 men, with 196 guns.

APPENDIX A.

B.—*Fortress Troops.*

Infantry.	Battalion.	Estimated Strength.
Nikolaievsk Fortress Infantry Battalion... ...	1	1,150

Artillery.	Companies.	Estimated Strength.
Port Arthur Fortress Artillery Regt. (2 Battalions)	8	2,620
Vladivostok Fortress Artillery Regt. (2 Battalions)	8	2,620
Nikolaievsk Fortress Artillery Company ...	1	392
Possiet Bay Fortress Artillery Detachment ...	1	327
Total Fortress Artillery	18	5,959

Engineers.	Companies.	Estimated Strength.
Vladivostok Fortress Sapper and Mining Company	1	236
Vladivostok Submarine Mining Company ...	1	165
Nikolaievsk Submarine Mining Company ...	1	88
Novokievskoe (Possiet Bay) Submarine Mining Company	1	88
Total Fortress Engineers	4	577

C.—*Railway Troops.*

—	Companies.	Estimated Strength.
Ussuri Railway Brigade—1st and 2nd Ussuri Railway Battalions	8	3,655
Trans-Amur Railway Brigade—4 Battalions ...	16	7,776
Total Railway Troops	24	11,431

(4718)

D.—*Frontier Guards.*

On the lines of communication and guarding the railway.	Estimated Strength.
Infantry.—55 Companies	13,750 Men.
Cavalry.—55 Squadrons	8,250 ,,
Artillery.—6 Batteries	1,440 ,, with 48 guns.
Total Frontier Guards...	23,440 ,, with 48 guns.

The troops enumerated above in detail may be summarized as follows:—

—	Estimated Strength.	Guns.
A.—Field troops	83,350	196
B.—Fortress troops	7,686	—
C.—Railway troops	11,431	—
D.—Frontier Guards	23,440	48
Estimated combatant strength of the Russian troops present, or in process of formation, east of Lake Baikal at the beginning of February, 1904.	125,907*	244 horse, field and mountain guns. 8 machine guns.

* This number includes 13,849 Artillery men and 3,277 Sappers.

The above force would be accompanied by some 16,000 to 17,000 non-combatants, forming an integral part of the troops, who, though not increasing the fighting strength, must be included in the ration strength of the army.

APPENDIX B (I).

APPENDIX B (I).

GEOGRAPHICAL DISTRIBUTION OF THE RUSSIAN FORCES IN MANCHURIA (EXCLUSIVE OF THE KUAN-TUNG PENINSULA) AT THE END OF APRIL, 1904.

MANCHURIAN ARMY.

Commander-in-Chief: General Kuropatkin.

I.—*Southern Group.*

Lieut.-General Stakelberg.

Locality and Commander.	Troops.	Battalions.	Squadrons.	Guns.	Remarks.
1. Newchuang (Major-General Kondratovich)	33rd and 36th East Siberian Rifle Regiments	6	—	—	[1] 2nd squadron.
	Primorsk Dragoon Regiment	—	1[1]	—	[2] 2nd and 4th batteries.
	9th East Siberian Rifle Artillery Brigade	—	—	16[2]	[3] For the defence of the fort at Newchuang. They were mostly old guns of various types.
	Guns[3]	—	—	14	[4] 1st squadron.
2. Kai-ping—Pu-lan-tien (Major-General Zikov)	34th and 35th East Siberian Rifle Regiments	6	—	—	[5] 1st and 3rd batteries.
	Primorsk Dragoon Regiment	—	1[4]	—	
	9th East Siberian Rifle Artillery Brigade	—	—	16[5]	

(4718) F 2

GEOGRAPHICAL DISTRIBUTION OF THE RUSSIAN FORCES IN MANCHURIA AT THE END OF APRIL, 1904—continued.

Locality and Commander.	Troops.	Battalions.	Squadrons.	Guns.	Remarks.
	I.—*Southern Group—continued.*				
Hsiung-yao-cheng and neighbourhood (Colonel Voronov)	2nd East Siberian Rifle Regiment	1[6]			[6] 1st battalion.
	Prinorsk Dragoon Regiment		3[7]		[7] 4th, 5th and 6th squadrons.
	1st East Siberian Rifle Artillery Brigade			4[8]	[8] Of the 1st battery. The other half battery was at Ta-shih-chiao.
	2nd Trans-Baikal Cossack Horse Battery			6	[9] 3rd squadron.
Fu-chou ... Pu-lan-tien (Lieutenant-Colonel Rantsov)	Prinorsk Dragoon Regiment		1[9]		[10] 1st battalion.
	4th East Siberian Rifle Regiment	1[10]			[11] The troops at Ta-shih-chiao were held as a general reserve.
3. Ta-shih-chiao[11] (Major-General Gerngross)	1st East Siberian Rifle Regiment	3			[12] One company was on the line of communication between Lao-yang and Feng-huang-cheng.
	2nd East Siberian Rifle Regiment	2			
	3rd East Siberian Rifle Regiment	2¾[12]			
	4th East Siberian Rifle Regiment	2			[13] 2nd, 3rd, 4th and half the 1st batteries.
	1st East Siberian Artillery Brigade			28[13]	
	II.—*Eastern Group.* Lieut.-General Zasulich.				
1. Coast line between Pi-tzu-wo and Lower Ya-lu (Major-General Mishchenko)	21st East Siberian Rifle Regiment	2¾[14]			[14] One company was still in the Ussuri District.
	24th East Siberian Rifle Regiment	¾[15]			[15] 9th and 10th companies; they were on the line of communication Hsiu-yen–Ta-ku-shan.
	1st Verkhne-Udinsk Cossack Regiment		5		
	1st Chita Cossack Regiment		6		
	1st Battery 6th East Siberian Rifle Artillery Brigade			8	
	1st Trans-Baikal Cossack Horse Battery			6	

APPENDIX B (I).

2. An-tung (Colonel Schwerin)	9th East Siberian Rifle Regiment	1^{16}	—	—
	10th East Siberian Rifle Regiment	$2\frac{3}{4}^{17}$	—	—
	24th East Siberian Rifle Regiment	$\frac{1}{4}^{18}$	—	—
	3rd East Siberian Rifle Artillery Brigade	—	—	16^{19}
3. Chiu-lien-cheng Detachment (Major-General Kashtalinskii) Chiu-lien-cheng	11th East Siberian Rifle Regiment	3^{19}	—	—
	12th East Siberian Rifle Regiment	$\frac{1}{4}^{20}$	—	—
	24th East Siberian Rifle Regiment		—	—
	6th East Siberian Rifle Artillery Brigade	—	—	—
	Machine Guns	—	—	8^{21}
Po-te-tien-tzu	11th East Siberian Rifle Regiment	1^{22}	—	8
	22nd East Siberian Rifle Regiment	2^{23}	—	—
	6th East Siberian Rifle Artillery Brigade	—	—	—
Ching-kou	22nd East Siberian Rifle Regiment	1^{25}	—	6^{24}
	6th East Siberian Rifle Artillery Brigade	—	—	—
Tien-tzu	9th East Siberian Rifle Regiment	2^{27}	—	2^{26}
	11th East Siberian Rifle Regiment	2^{28}	—	—
	3rd East Siberian Rifle Artillery Brigade	—	—	—
4. An-ping-ho Detachment[30] (Colonel Lechitski)	10th East Siberian Rifle Regiment	$\frac{1}{4}^{31}$	—	8^{29}
	24th East Siberian Rifle Regiment	1^{32}	—	—
	Ussuri Cossack Regiment	—	2^{33}	—
	1st East Siberian Mountain Battery	—	—	6
Pu-hsi Ho Detachment (Colonel Kartsev)	Ussuri Cossack Regiment	—	3^{34}	—
Kuan-tien-cheng (Colonel Trukhin)	1st Argun Cossack Regiment	—	^{35}	—
	1st Argun Cossack Regiment	—	$4\frac{1}{2}^{36}$	2 (mountain)
4. Feng-huang-cheng	24th East Siberian Rifle Regiment	$\frac{1}{2}^{37}$	—	—
	23rd East Siberian Rifle Regiment	3	—	—
	2nd Chita Cossack Regiment	—	4^{38}	—
5. *En route* from Liao-yang to join the Eastern Group	3rd East Siberian Rifle Artillery Brigade	—	—	8^{39}
	6th East Siberian Rifle Artillery Brigade	—	—	8^{40}

[15] 2nd battalion.
[17] 10 and 11th companies.
[18] 1st and 2nd batteries.
[19] 5th, 6th and 8th companies.
[20] 8th company.
[21] 2nd battery.
[22] 7th company.
[23] 2nd and 3rd battalions.
[24] 3rd battery.
[25] 1st battalion.
[26] 3rd battery.
[27] 1st and 3rd battalions.
[28] 1st and 3rd battalions.
[29] 3rd battery.
[30] This detachment left An-ping-ho on 29th April, and retired up the valley of the An-ping River towards Hung-shih-lā.
[31] 10th company.
[32] 1st battalion.
[33] 1st and 2nd squadrons.
[34] 3rd, 4th and 5th squadrons.
[35] 5th squadron.
[36] The other half squadron was detained on the line of communication An-tung – Feng-huang-cheng, as postal orderlies. Colonel Trukhin was under the orders of Colonel Kartsev.
[37] 5th and 6th companies. They were retained as a garrison for that city.
[38] These 4 squadrons had reached Feng-huang-cheng on 29th April.
[39] 4th battery.
[40] 4th battery.

GEOGRAPHICAL DISTRIBUTION OF THE RUSSIAN FORCES IN MANCHURIA AT THE END OF APRIL, 1904—continued.

Locality and Commander.	Troops.	Battalions.	Squadrons.	Guns.	Remarks.
III.—Army Reserve.					
1. Hai-cheng	18th East Siberian Rifle Regiment	2[41]	—	—	[41] 1st and 3rd battalions.
	17th East Siberian Rifle Regiment	3	—	—	[42] 2nd and 3rd battalions.
2. An-shan-chan	19th East Siberian Rifle Regiment	3	—	—	[43] The other two guns were with Major-General Kossakovski, on the Liao Ho.
	20th East Siberian Rifle Regiment	2[42]	—	—	
	5th East Siberian Rifle Artillery Brigade	—	—	32	[44] 2nd battalion, employed on road-mending.
	2nd Chita Cossack Regiment	—	1	—	[45] 1st battalion, on lines of communication.
3. Railway line between An-shan-chan and Liao-yang (Major-General Rennenkampf)	2nd Verkhne-Udinsk Cossack Regiment	—	6	—	[46] On line of communication.
	2nd Nerchinsk Cossack Regiment	—	6	—	[47] 3rd battalion, or: road-mending.
	3rd and 4th Trans-Baikal Cossack Horse Batteries	—	—	12	[48] 7th company, on road-mending.
	123rd Koslov Regiment	3	—	—	[49] 4th battalion, on road-mending.
	124th Voronej Regiment	3	—	—	[50] 3rd battalion.
	139th Morshansk Regiment	3	—	—	[51] 1st 2nd, 6th and 7th companies.
4. Liao-yang	140th Zaraisk Regiment	3	—	—	[52] Belonging to the 4th battery.
	Amur Cossack Regiment	—	1½	—	[53] This detachment was for the personal protection of the Viceroy Alexeiev, and was not under General Kuropatkin's orders.
	2nd Chita Cossack Regiment	—	1	—	
	31st Artillery Brigade	—	—	22[53]	
	35th Artillery Brigade	1	—	24	

APPENDIX B (I).

IV.—Troops Employed on Special Duties.

1. Between Hai-cheng and Hsiu-yen	18th East Siberian Rifle Regiment	1[44]
	20th East Siberian Rifle Regiment	1[45]
2. Between Liao-yang an Feng-huang-cheng	3rd East Siberian Rifle Regiment	½[46]
	140th Zaraisk Regiment	1[47]
3. East Fen-shui Ling	24th East Siberian Rifle Regiment	¼[48]
	124th Voronej Regiment	1[49]
4. Mo-tien Ling	139th Morshansk Regiment	1[50]

V.—Other Troops.

1. On the Liao Ho, between Tien-chuang-tai and Hsin-min-tun, with headquarters at Ta-wan (Major-General Kossakovski)	123rd Koslov Regiment	1[51]
	Amur Cossack Regiment	3½
	31st Artillery Brigade	
2. Mukden[53]	1st Strietensk Infantry Regiment	2
	Amur Cossack Regiment	½
3. Harbin	1st Siberian Infantry Division[54]	14
	1st Siberian Artillery Brigade	
4. Hsing-ching	Amur Cossack Regiment	½
5. Upper Ya-lu	Ussuri Cossack Regiment	1

[54] Consisting of :—1st Strietensk Regiment (2 battalions), 2nd Chita Infantry Regiment (4 battalions), 3rd Nerchinsk Regiment (4 battalions, *en route* from Trans-Baikalia), 4th Verkhne-Udinsk Infantry Regiment (4 battalions). This force was retained as a special reserve in Harbin, at the specific request of the Viceroy, without the consent of General Kuropatkin. It was intended as a re-inforcement to South Manchuria, or to Vladivostok, as occasion might arise.

2[52]

32

Note.—*The Engineer Troops* (1st, 2nd and 3rd East Siberian Sapper Battalions), consisting of 9 sapper companies, 2½ telegraph companies, and 2 pontoon companies, and the *Frontier Guards* have not been included in this table ; they were scattered about the country in small detachments. For the troops in the Kuan-tung Peninsula and Ussuri District, see Appendix B (II).

APPENDIX B (II).

STRENGTH AND

1. *Southern Group.*
Lieut.-General Stakelberg.

1st E. Sib. Rifle Div.		9th E. Sib. Rifle Div.	
1st Bde.	2nd Bde.	1st Bde.	2nd Bde.
1. ■■■	3.* ■■■	33. ■■■	35. ■■■
2. ■■■	4. ■■■	34. ■■■	36. ■■■

1st E. Sib. Rifle Art. Bde. ılı ılı ılı ılı
9th E. Sib. Art. Bde. ılı ılı ılı ılı

Primorsk Dragoon Regt.

2nd Trans-Baikal Cossack Horse Battery. ılı (6 guns.)

	Rifles.	Sabres.	Guns.
Total	16,600	720	70†

2. *Eastern Group.*
Lieut.-General Zasulich.

3rd E. Sib. Rifle Div.		6th E. Sib. Rifle Div.	
1st Bde.	2nd Bde.	1st Bde.	2nd Bde.
9. ■■■	11. ■■■	21.* ■■■	23.† □□□
10. ■■■	12. ■■■	22. ■■■	24.‡ ■■■

3rd E. Sib. Rifle Art. Bde. ılı ılı ılı ılı §
6th E. Sib. Rifle Art. Bde. ılı ılı ılı ılı §

1st E. Sib. Mountain Battery. ılı (6 guns.)

½ 2nd E. Sib. Sapper Battalion.

Trans-Baikal Cossack Bde.
Maj.-Gen. Mishchenko.

1st. Verkhne-Udinsk Regt. (5 squadrons.)
1st Chita Regt.
2nd Chita Regt. (4 squadrons.)

Ussuri Cossack Regt. (5 squadrons.)
1st Argun Cossack Regt. (with 2 mountain guns.)
Horse Battery. ılı (6 guns.)

	Rifles.	Sabres.	Guns.
Total	16,450	3,120	78 and 8 machine guns.

Grand total in

---

* 1 company on line of communication between Liao-yang and Feng-huang-cheng.
† This number does not include the 14 guns of position of various types used in the defences of Newchuang, mentioned in Appendix B. (I).

* Less 1 company in the Ussuri District.
† *En route* from Liao-yang to join the Eastern Group; they are included in the total, however.
‡ Less 1 company on special duty. See also Appendix B. (I).
§ The 4th batteries of these 2 brigades were *en route* from Liao-yang.

COMPOSITION OF THE RUSSIAN COMBATANT FORCES IN

Commander-in-Chief of the Land and

A.—MANCHURIAN ARMY.

Commander-in-Chief :—General Kuropatkin.

1st Siberian Army Corps.   IInd Siberian Army Corps.
Lieut.-General Stakelberg.   Lieut.-General Zasulic

The troops were grouped without reference to the above Army

In Manchuria (exclusive of the Kuan-tung Peninsula).

3. *Army Reserve.*

5th E. Sib. Rifle Div.   2 Bde.   2 Bde.
(Maj.-Gen. Alexeiev.)   31st Inf. Div.   35th Inf. Div.
    (Maj.-Gen.   (Maj.-Gen.
1st Bde.   2nd Bde.   Vassiliev.)   Glasko.)
17.   19.   123.*   139.†
■ ■ ■   ■ ■ ■   ■ ■ ■ ■   ■ ■ ■ ■
18.†   20.†   124.†   140.†
■ □ ■   □ ■ ■   ■ ■ ■ □   ■ ■ □ ■

5th E.Sib.Rifle Art.Bde.   2/31stArt.Bde.*   2/35thArt.Bde.
╷╷╷ ╷╷╷ ╷╷╷ ╷╷╷   ╷╷╷ ╷╷╷ ╷╷╷   ╷╷╷ ╷╷╷ ╷╷╷

2nd Chita Cossack Regt.   Amur Cossack Regt.
⚑ (1 squadron.)   ⚑ (1½ squadron.)

East Siberian Sapper Battalions.
½ 1st.   ½ 2nd.   3rd.
■   ■   ■

Trans-Baikal Cossack Division.
(Maj.-Gen. Rennenkampf.)
2nd Verkhne-Udinsk Regt.   2nd Nerchinsk Regt.
⚑   ⚑

2nd Argun Regt.   2nd Chita Regt.
⚑   ⚑ (1 squadron.)

3rd and 4th Trans-Baikal Cossack Horse Batteries.
╷╷╷ ╷╷╷ (12 guns.)

	Rifles.	Sabres.	Guns.
Total	15,400	2,580	90

4. *Troops Employed*

139th (Morshansk) Regt.
■ (1 battalion.) ■

124th (Voronej) Regt.
■ (1 battalion.)

3rd E. Sib. Rifle Regt.
■ (1 company.) ■

20th E. Sib. Rifle Regt.
■ (1 battalion.) ■

	Rifles.
Total	3,850

	Rifles.	Sabres.	Guns.
Manchuria	64,200	7,080	272

* 4 companies and 2 guns with Maj.-Gen. Kos-akovski, on the Liao Ho.
† 1 battalion of each of these regiments was on special duty. See also Appendix B. (I).

APPENDIX B (II).

THE FAR EAST AT THE END OF APRIL, 1904 (EXCLUSIVE OF FORTRESS

NAVAL FORCES IN THE FAR EAST :— VICEROY ADMIRAL ALEXEIEV.

IIIrd SIBERIAN ARMY CORPS.
Lieut.-General Stessel.

Corps as follows: —

on Special Duties.	5. *Other Troops.*	KUAN-TUNG PENINSULA
		Commander
140th (Zaraisk) Regt. ■ (1 battalion.)	1st Sib. Infantry Division. (Maj.-Gen. Morosov.)	4th E. Sib. Rifle Div. (Maj.-Gen. Fock.)
	1st (Strietensk.) ■■■■ 2nd (Chita) ■■■■	1st. Bde. 2nd Bde.
	3rd (Nerchinsk.)* ■■■■ 4th (Verkhne-Udinsk). ■■■■	13. ■■■ 15. ■■■
		14. ■■■ 16. ■■■
18th E. Sib. Rifle Regt. ■ (1 battalion.)	123rd (Koslov) Regt. ■ (4 companies.)	4th E. Sib. Rifle Art. Bde. ╎╎ ╎╎ ╎╎ ╎╎
24th E. Sib. Rifle Regt. ■ (1 company.)	1st Sib. Art. Bde. ╎╎ ╎╎ ╎╎ ╎╎ 2/31st Art. Bde. ╎╎ (2 guns.)	
		1st
	Amur Cossack Regt. ⚑ (4½ squadrons.)	
	† Ussuri Cossack Regt. ⚑ (1 squadron.)	Kuan-
	Mounted Detachments of the 1st and 15th E. Sib. Rifle Regts. and some Caucasian Volunteers.	
Sabres. Guns. — —	Rifles. Sabres. Guns. Total ... 11,900 660 34	Grand total ...

* *En route* from Trans-Baikalia.

† With Colonel Madritov on the Upper Ya-lu.

* From the 2nd E. Sib. 1st Company which formed

AND TECHNICAL TROOPS).

	B.—USSURI DISTRICT.
(Port Arthur and neighbourhood).	(Lieut.-General Linevich.)

—Lieut.-General Stessel.

Port Arthur side (left column)

7th E. Sib. Rifle Div.
(Maj.-Gen. Kondratenko.)

1st Bde.	2nd Bde.	E. Sib. Rifle Regt.
25. ■■■	27. ■■■	5.* ■■■
26. ■■■	28. ■■■	

7th E. Sib. Rifle Art. Bde.
∥ ∥ ∥

Verkhne-Udinsk Regt.
⚑ (1 squadron.)

tung Sapper Company.
■

Ussuri District (right column)

2nd E. Sib. Rifle Div.

1st Bde.	2nd Bde
5.* □□□	7. ■■■
6. ■■■	8. ■■■

8th E. Sib. Rifle Div.

1st Bde.	2nd Bde.
29. ■■■	31. ■■■
30. ■■■	32. ■■■

2nd E. Sib. Art. Bde.
∥ ∥ ∥ ∥

8th E. Sib. Art. Bde.
∥ ∥ ∥

Independent Amur Cossack Div.   1st Nerchinsk Cossack Regt.
⚑ (3 squadrons.)   ⚑

∥ ∥ 2 mountain batteries.

½ 1st E. Sib. Sapper Battalion.
■

	Rifles.	Sabres.	Guns.
	25,000	120	56
Grand total	14,700	1,080	12

* In the Kuan-tung Peninsula.

Remarks.

In the totals, the strengths have been estimated as per Appendix A, except the infantry in the Kuan-tung Peninsula which was nearly up to full strength.

The Frontier Guards, numbering approximately 13,750 rifles, 8,250 sabres, and 48 guns, have not been included in this Table. They were scattered over the country in small detachments.

Rifle Division in the Ussuri District, less the part of the Legation Guard at Peking.

APPENDIX C.

ORDER OF BATTLE

OF THE JAPANESE FIRST ARMY ON THE 1ST MAY, 1904.

General Officer Commanding : General Baron Kuroki.
Chief of the Staff: Major-General Fuji.
Commander of Artillery : Colonel Matsumoto.
Commander of Engineers : Major-General T. Kodama.

	Battalions.	Squadrons.	Guns.	Engineer Companies.
GUARD DIVISION.				
Commander: Lieutenant-General Baron Hashegawa.				
1st Guard Brigade, Major-General N. Asada.				
1st Guard Regiment	3	—	—	—
2nd Guard Regiment	3	—	—	—
2nd Guard Brigade, Major-General A. Watanabe.				
3rd Guard Regiment	3	—	—	—
4th Guard Regiment	3	—	—	—
CAVALRY.				
Guard Cavalry Regiment	—	3	—	—
ARTILLERY.				
Guard Artillery Regiment (field guns)	—	—	36	—
ENGINEERS.				
Guard Engineer Battalion	—	—	—	3

APPENDIX C.

ORDER OF BATTLE—*Continued.*

	Battalions.	Squadrons.	Guns.	Engineer Companies.
2ND DIVISION.				
Commander: Lieutenant-General Baron Nishi.				
3rd Brigade, Major-General M. Matsunaga.				
4th Regiment	3	—	—	—
29th Regiment	3	—	—	—
15th Brigade, Major-General S. Okasaki.				
16th Regiment	3	—	—	—
30th Regiment	3	—	—	—
CAVALRY.				
2nd Cavalry Regiment	—	3	—	—
ARTILLERY.				
2nd Artillery Regiment (field guns)	—	—	36	—
ENGINEERS.				
2nd Engineer Battalion	—	—	—	3
12TH DIVISION.				
Commander: Lieutenant-General Baron Inouye.				
12th Brigade, Major-General N. Sasaki.				
14th Regiment	3	—	—	—
47th Regiment	3	—	—	—
23rd Brigade, Major-General Kigoshi.				
24th Regiment	3	—	—	—
46th Regiment	3	—	—	—
CAVALRY.				
12th Cavalry Regiment	—	3	—	—
ARTILLERY.				
12th Artillery Regiment (mountain guns)	—	—	36	—

Order of Battle—*Continued.*

	Battalions.	Squadrons.	Guns.	Engineer Companies.
ENGINEERS.				
12th Engineer Battalion	—	—	—	3
CORPS ARTILLERY.				
5 Howitzer batteries (4·72-in. Krupp)	—	—	20	—
Total	36		128	9

Note.—The strength of a battalion of infantry may be taken at about 800, and of a squadron of cavalry at about 140.

APPENDIX C.

ORDER OF BATTLE

OF THE RUSSIAN EASTERN FORCE ON THE 1ST MAY, 1904.

General Officer Commanding: Lieutenant-General Zasulich (commanding 2nd Siberian Army Corps).

Chief of the Staff: Colonel Oranovski.

	Battalions.	Squadrons.	Guns.	Engineer Companies.
3RD EAST SIBERIAN RIFLE DIVISION.				
Commander: Major-General Kashtalinski.				
1st Brigade, Major-General Mardanov.				
9th East Siberian Rifle Regiment	3	—	—	—
10th East Siberian Rifle Regiment	3	—	—	—
2nd Brigade, Major-General Stolitza.				
11th East Siberian Rifle Regiment	3	—	—	—
12th East Siberian Rifle Regiment	3	—	—	—
Machine Gun Company, attached to 9th East Siberian Rifle Regiment.	—	—	8	—
ARTILLERY.				
East Siberian Rifle Artillery Brigade, Colonel Shwerin.				
1st, 2nd, and 3rd Batteries	—	—	24	—
6TH EAST SIBERIAN RIFLE DIVISION.				
Commander: Major-General Trusov.				
1st Brigade, Major-General Yatsinin.				
21st East Siberian Rifle Regiment	3	—	—	—
22nd East Siberian Rifle Regiment	3	—	—	—
2nd Brigade, Major-General Krechinski.				
23rd East Siberian Rifle Regiment	3	—	—	—
24th East Siberian Rifle Regiment	3	—	—	—
ARTILLERY.				
6th East Siberian Rifle Artillery Brigade, Colonel Meister.				
2nd, and 3rd Batteries	—	—	16	—

ORDER OF BATTLE.—*Continued.*

	Battalions.	Squadrons.	Guns.	Engineer Companies.
ENGINEERS.				
2nd Company, 2nd East Siberian Sapper Battalion	—	—	—	1
CAVALRY.				
Trans-Baikal Cossack Brigade, Major-General Mishchenko.				
1st Verkhne-Udinsk Trans-Baikal Cossack Regiment	—	6	—	
1st Chita Trans-Baikal Cossack Regiment	—	6	—	
Attached.				
1st Arguu Trans-Baikal Cossack Regiment	—	6	—	—
Ussuri Cossack Regiment	—	5	—	—
1st Trans-Baikal Cossack Horse Battery	—	—	6	—
1st East Siberian Mountain Battery	—	—	8	—
Total	24	24	54	1

The total combatant strength of this force amounted to about 21,000 men, of which the infantry was nearly 17,000.

Note.—All of the above force was not present on the Ya-lu on the 1st May, 1904.

2¾ battalions of the 21st East Siberian Rifle Regiment were in the neighbourhood of Ta-ku-shan.

The 23rd East Siberian Rifle Regiment left Liao-yang for the Ya-lu on the 30th April.

Five Companies of the 24th East Siberian Rifle Regiment and one company of the 10th East Siberian Rifle Regiment were on the line of communication.

The 1st Verkhne-Udinsk and 1st Chita Cossack Regiments were engaged in watching the coast from the mouth of the Ya-lu westward, and with it were a horse battery and a battery of field guns.

The mountain battery with the Russian troops at Chang-tien-cheng (see p. 53) was the 1st East Siberian Mountain Battery, transferred from Major-General Mishchenko's force and replaced by the 1st/6th Battery.

LOSSES AT THE BATTLE OF THE YA-LU.

Japanese.

The following statement is from Japanese sources, and includes losses from the 26th April to 1st May.

Killed.		Wounded.		Missing.		Total Losses.		
Officers.	Other ranks.	Officers.	Other ranks.	Officers.	Other ranks.	Officers.	Other ranks.	Grand Total.
5	198	33	775	—	10	38	983	1,021

An Austrian authority gives the losses by divisions as shown in the table below. It will be noticed that there is a discrepancy of 49 between the two statements.

Body of Troops.	Killed.		Wounded.		Total Losses.		
	Officers.	Other ranks.	Officers.	Other ranks.	Officers.	Other ranks.	Grand Total.
Guard Division ...	1	25	7	146	8	171	179
2nd ,, ...	1	90	14	352	15	442	457
12th ,, ...	3	48	8	375	11	423	434
	5	163	29	873	34	1,036	1,070

Russian.

The statement given below is a compilation from two Russian tables of losses, and is greatly at variance with the computation of the Japanese, who assert that up to the 7th May they buried 1,363 Russian dead. The Japanese estimate agrees more nearly with a less detailed Russian report, which gives the losses as 1,400 killed, and 1,100 wounded, and 600 missing.

Body of Troops.	Killed.		Wounded.		Missing.		Total Losses.		
	Officers.	Other ranks.	Officers.	Other ranks.	Officers.	Other ranks.	Officers.	Other ranks.	Grand Total.
Staff	1	—	1	—	—	—	2	—	2
9th Regiment ...	1	—	—	—	—	—	1	—	1
10th ,, ...	—	3	—	9	—	—	—	12	12
11th ,, ...	14	209	15	392	—	281	29	882	911
12th ,, ...	11	277	10	434	2	212	23	923	946
22th ,, ...	—	23	4	152	—	144	4	319	323
Artillery Staff ...	—	—	2	—	—	—	2	—	2
2nd/6th Battery ...	2	32	1	39	—	27	3	98	101
3rd/6th ,, ...	—	8	1	17	—	15	1	40	41
3rd/3rd ,, ...	3	24	2	58	—	—	5	82	87
Machine Gun Co. ...	1	16	1	38	—	—	2	54	56
2nd/2nd Sapper Co	—	—	1	1	—	—	1	1	2
	33	592	38	1,140	2	679	73	2,411	2,484

The 3rd/3rd Battery had 84 per cent. of its horses disabled and an almost similar loss befell the 2nd/6th Battery.

The Machine-Gun Company had twenty-two out of twenty-four horses disabled.

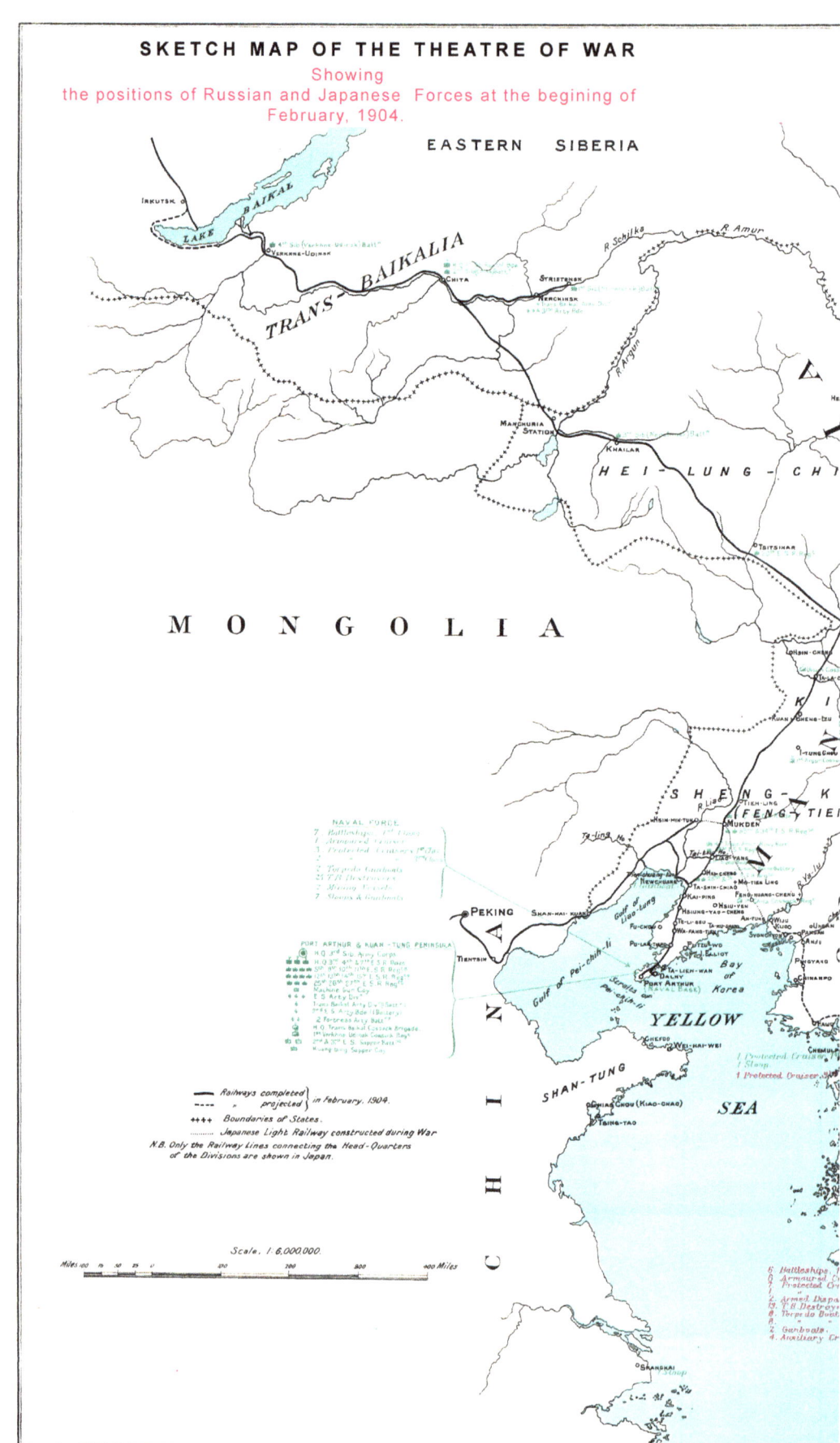

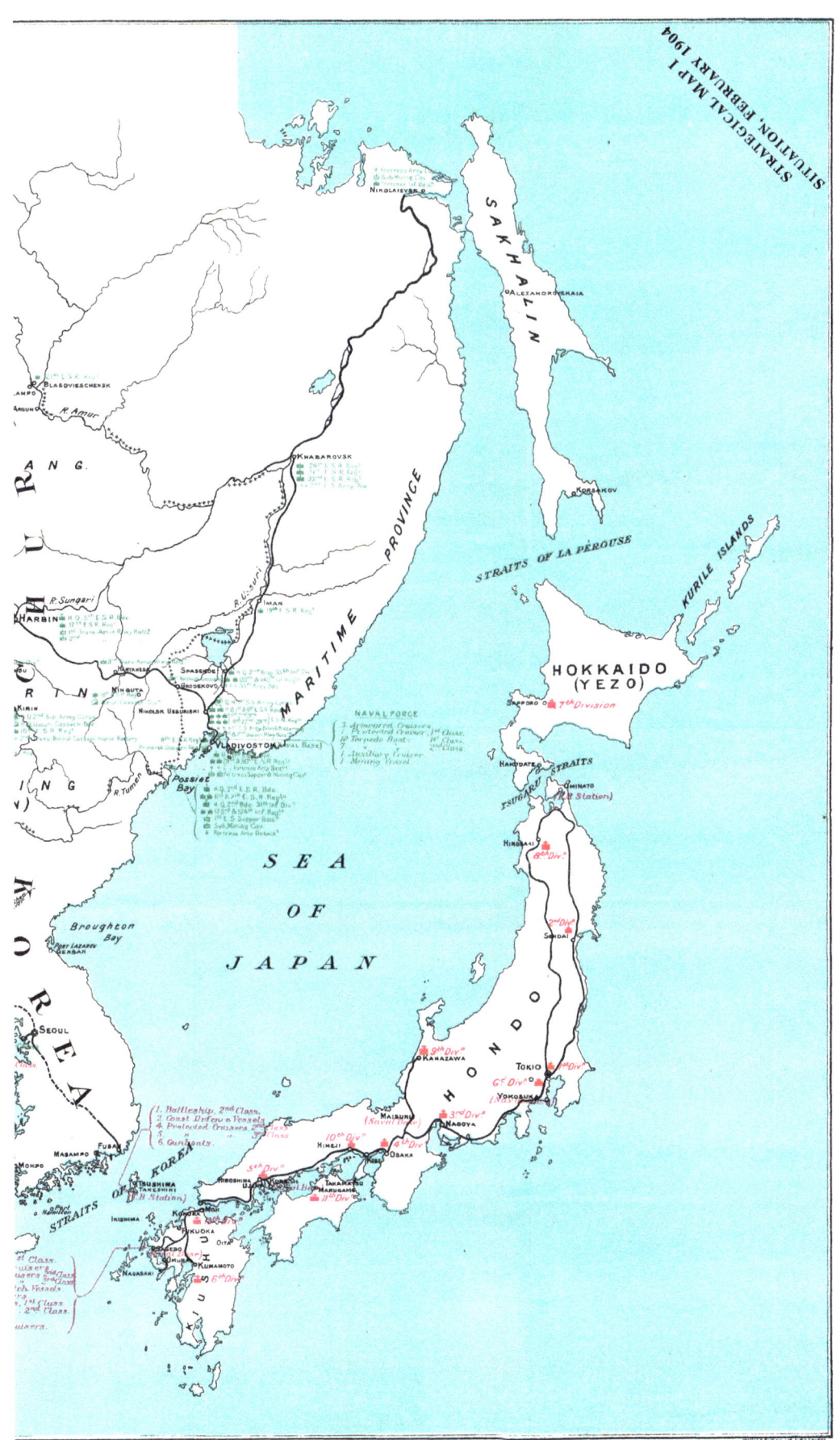

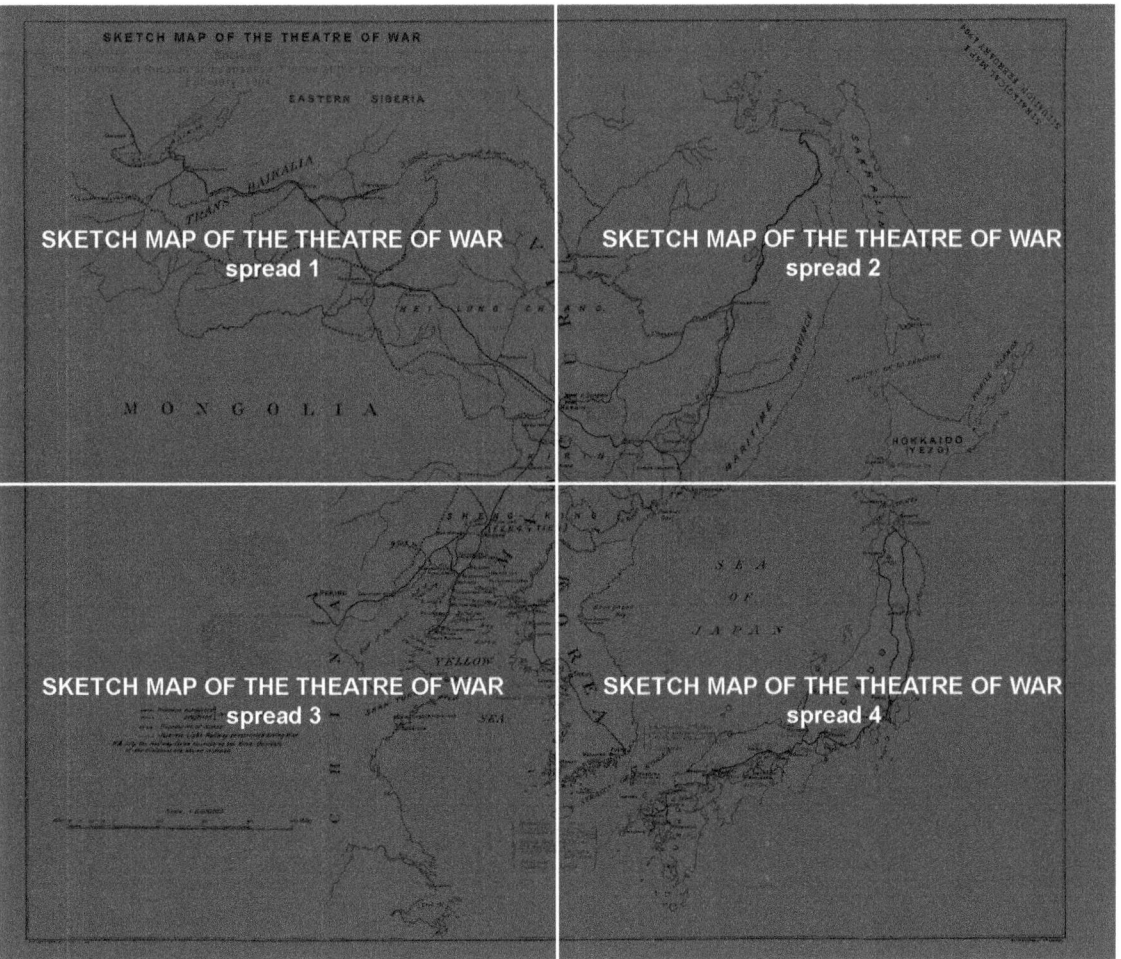

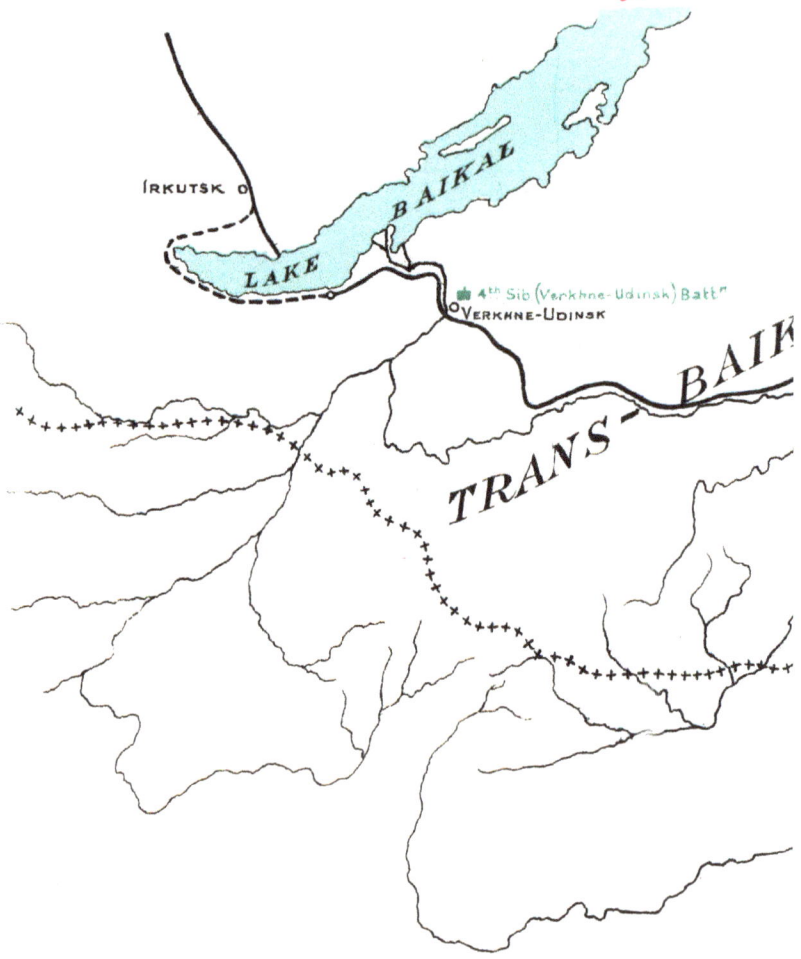

SKETCH MAP OF THE

Showing
the positions of Russian and Japanese
February, 1904.

THEATRE OF WAR

Forces at the begining of

EASTERN SIBERIA

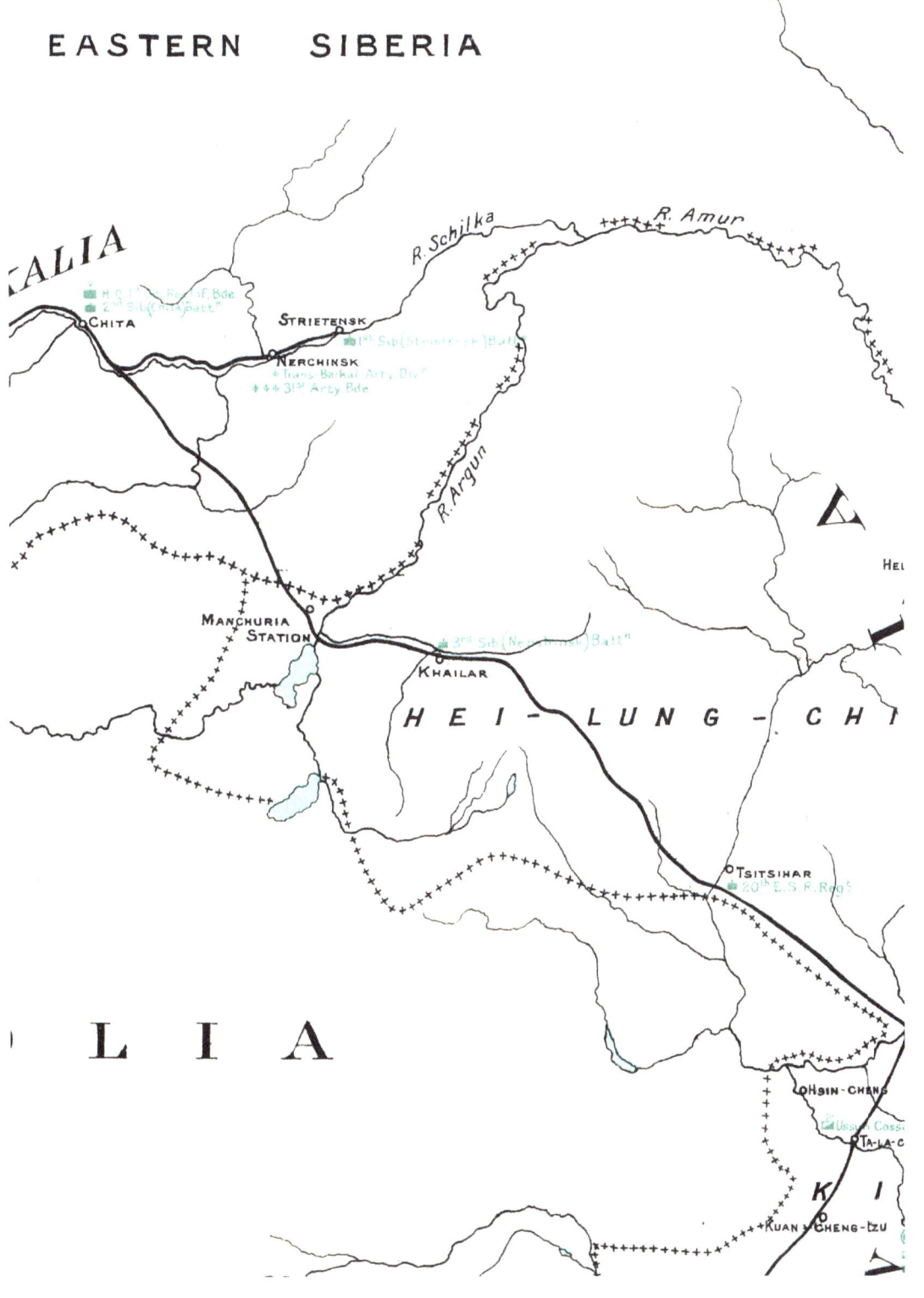

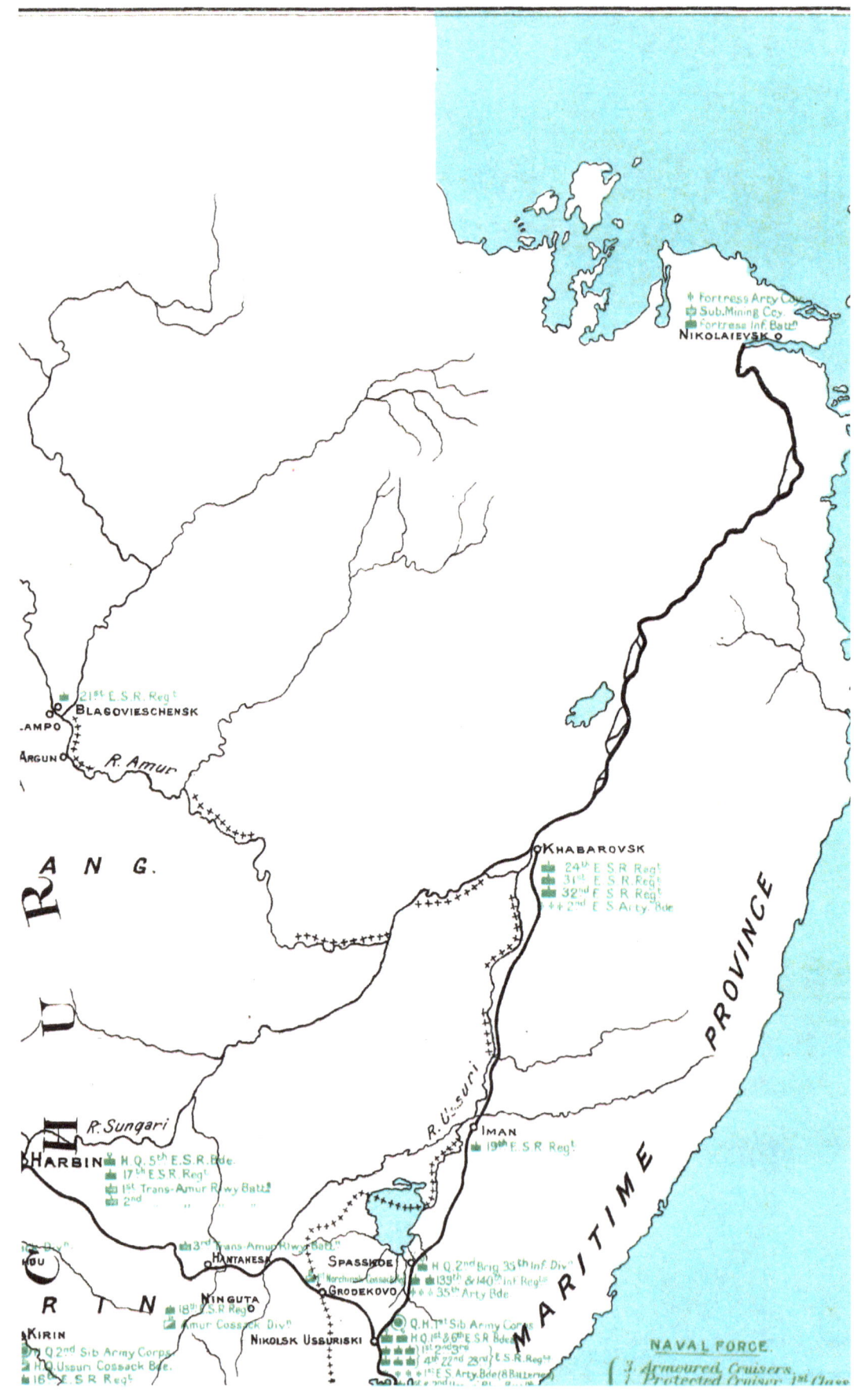

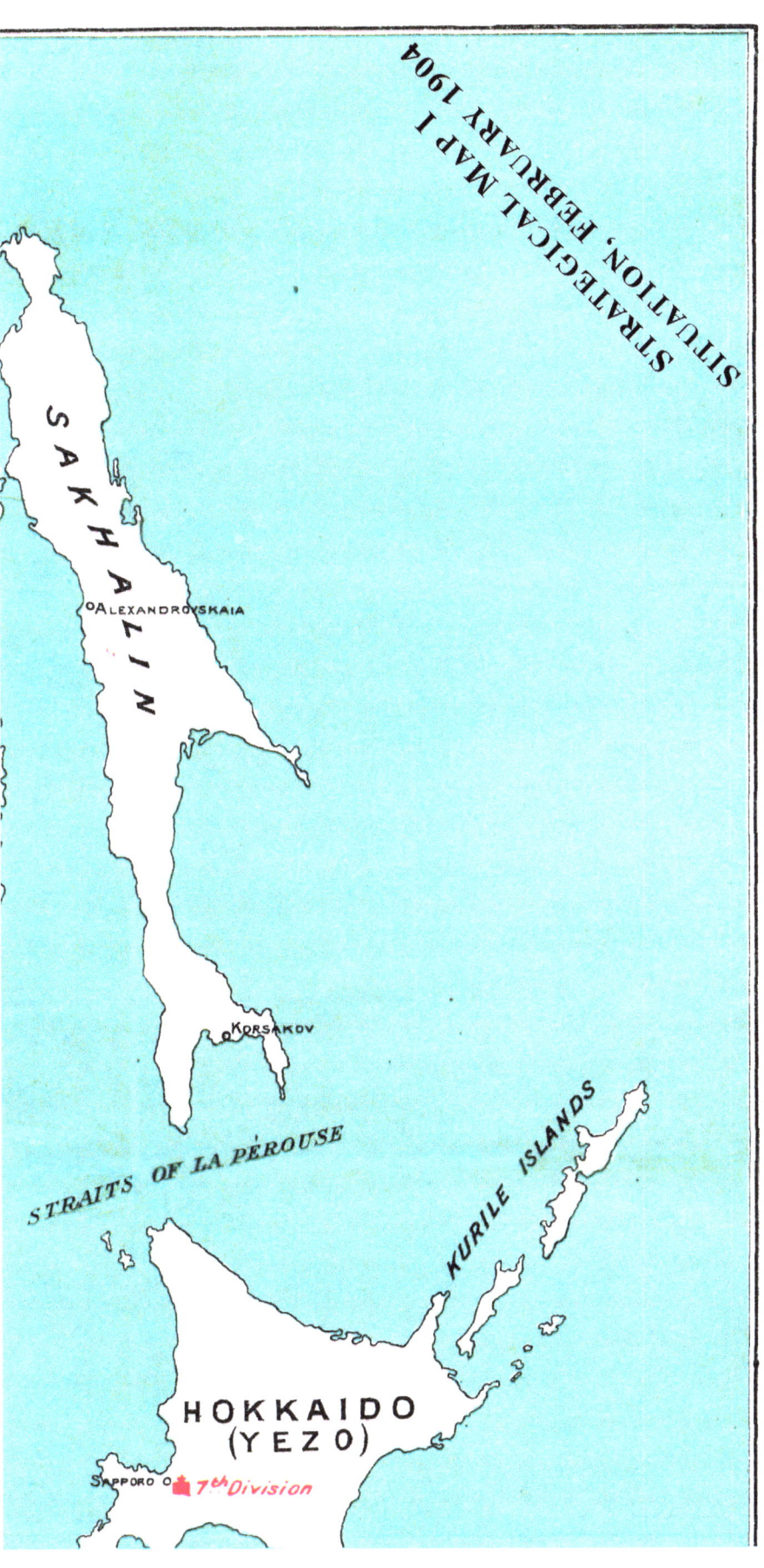

NAVAL FORCE

7. Battleships, 1st Cl
1. Armoured Cruiser
3. Protected Cruiser
2. "   "
2. Torpedo Gunboats.
25. T.B Destroyers.
2. Mining Vessels.
7. Sloops & Gunboats.

PORT ARTHUR & KUAN-TUN

- H.Q. 3rd Sib. Army Corps.
- H.Q. 3rd 4th & 7th E.S.R. Bdes
- 5th, 9th 10th 11th E.S.R. Regts
- 12th 13th 14th 15th E.S.R. Regts
- 25th 26th 27th E.S.R. Regts
- Machine Gun Coy.
- E.S. Arty Divn
- Trans-Baikal Arty Divn (I Batty)
- 2nd E.S. Arty Bde. (I Battery)
- 2 Fortress Arty. Batts
- H.Q. Trans-Baikal Cossack Brig
- 1st Verkhne-Udinsk Cossack Reg
- 2nd & 3rd E.S. Sapper Battns
- Kuang-tung Sapper Coy

—— Railways completed
---- "   projected } in February, 1904.
++++ Boundaries of States.
.... Japanese Light Railway constructed durin

N.B. Only the Railway Lines connecting the Head-Quarter of the Divisions are shown in Japan.

Scale, 1:6,000,000.

Miles 100 75 50 25 0   100   200   300

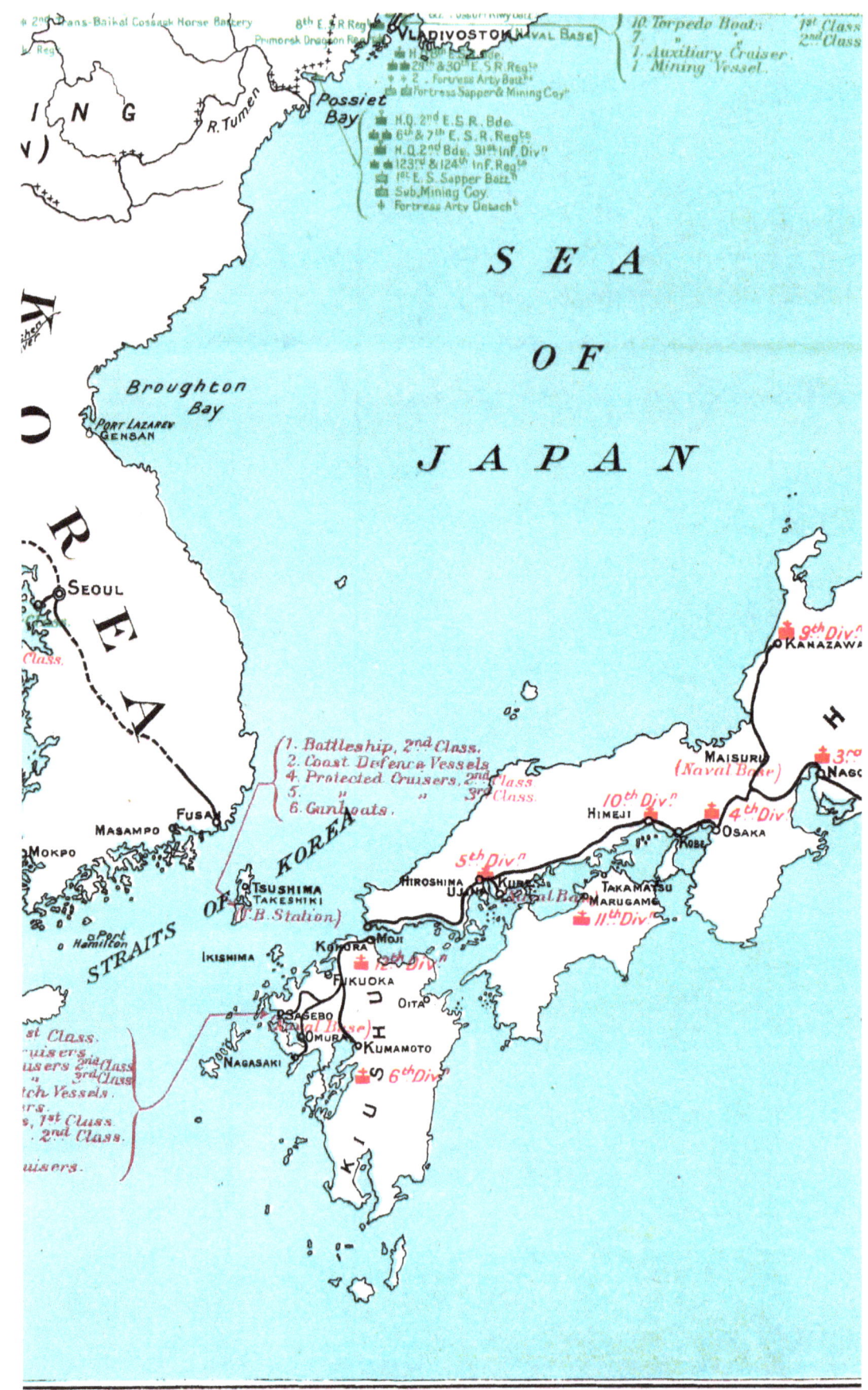

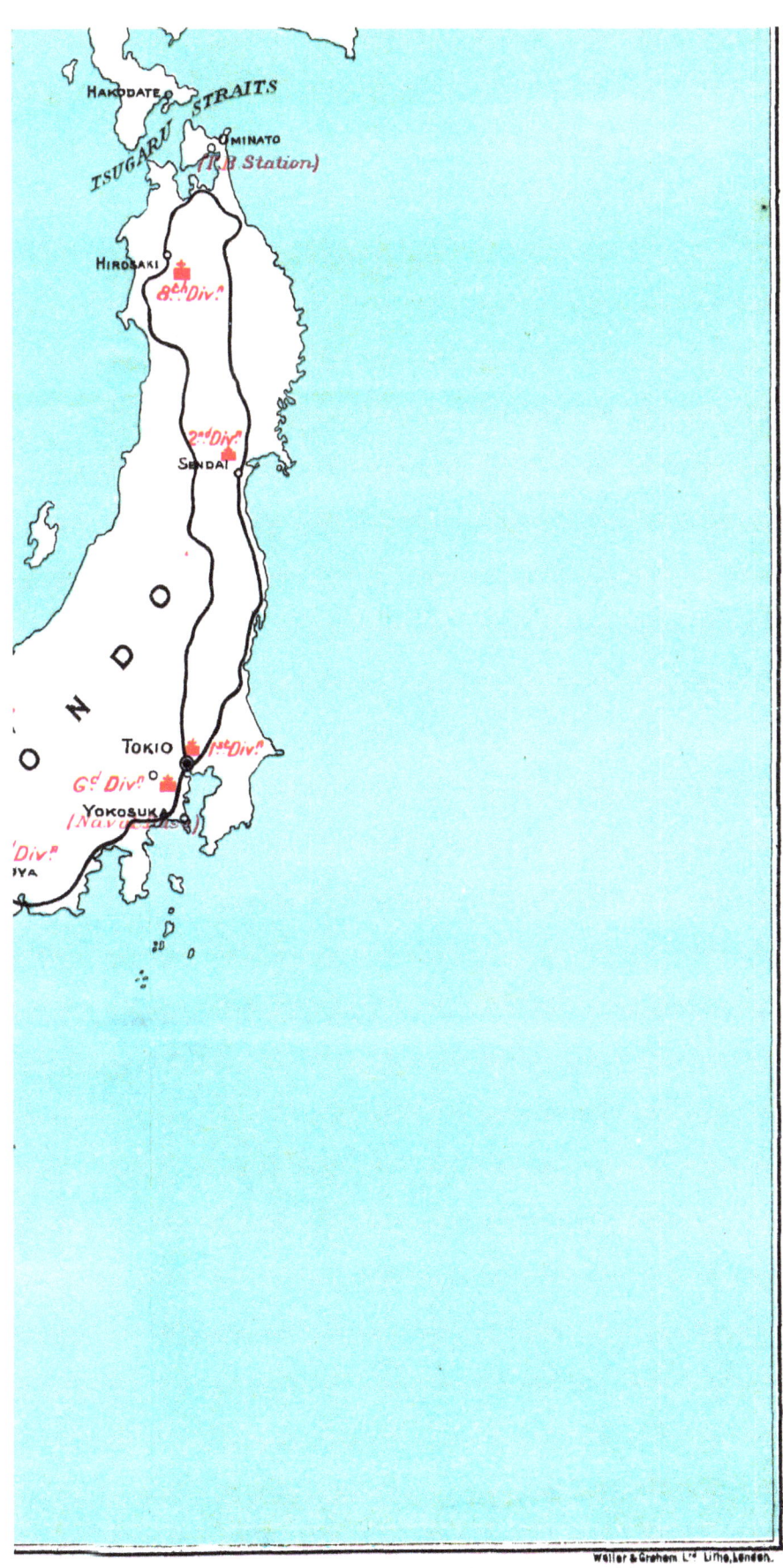

SKETCH MAP OF THE THEATRE OF WAR, 1904.

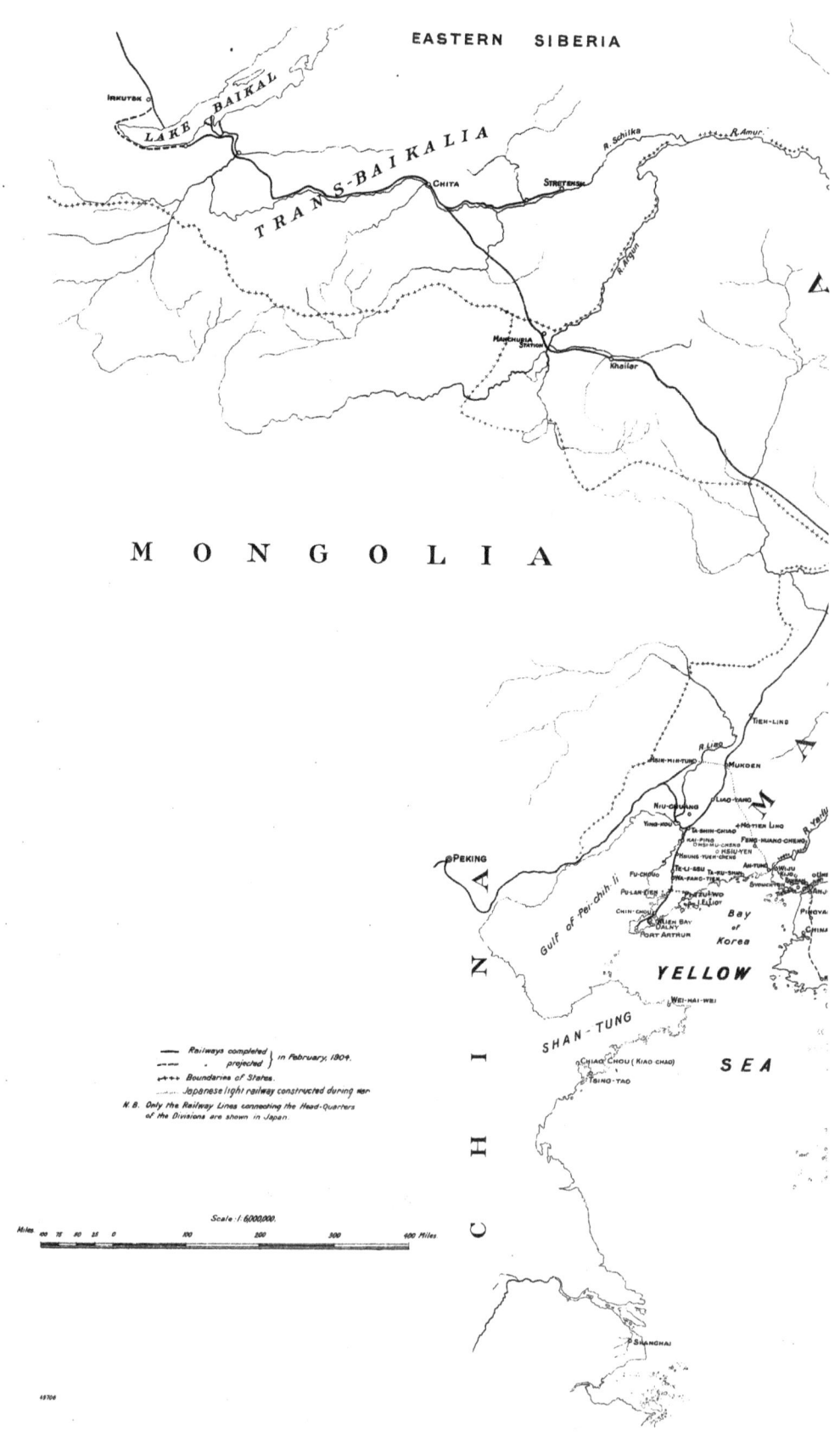

Map 1.

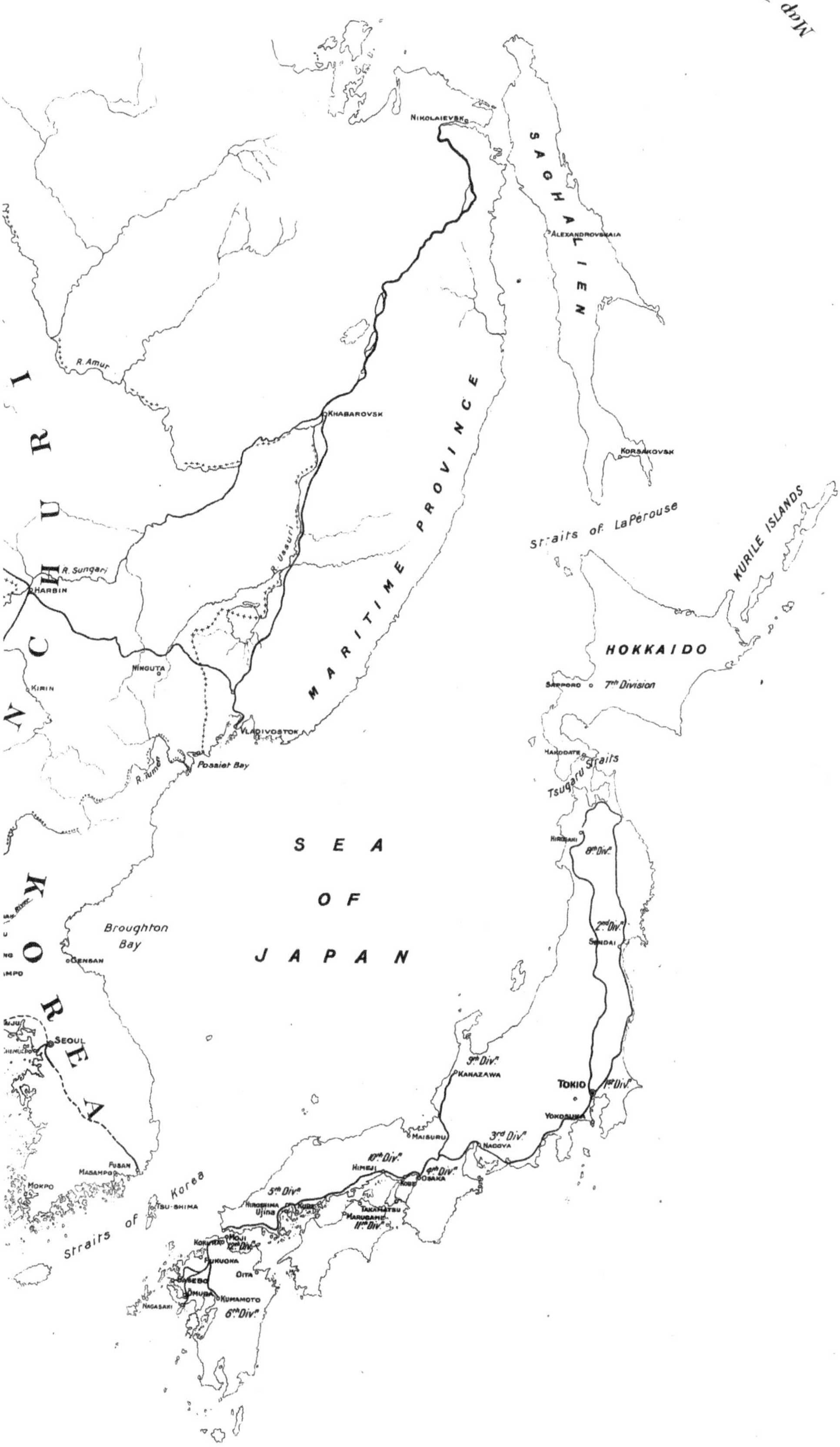
NIKOLAIEVSK
SAGHALIEN
ALEXANDROVSKAIA
KORSAKOVSK
R. Amur
KHABAROVSK
MARITIME PROVINCE
MANCHURIA
R. Sungari
HARBIN
R. Ussuri
NINGUTA
KIRIN
VLADIVOSTOK
Possiet Bay
R. Tumen
Straits of LaPérouse
KURILE ISLANDS
HOKKAIDO
SAPPORO
7th Division
HAKODATE
Tsugaru Straits
HIROSAKI
8th Divn
2nd Divn
SENDAI
SEA OF JAPAN
Broughton Bay
GENSAN
KOREA
SEOUL
CHEMULPO
9th Divn
KANAZAWA
TOKIO
1st Divn
YOKOSUKA
3rd Divn
NAGOYA
MAISURU
10th Divn
HIMEJI
4th Divn
OSAKA
KOBE
5th Divn
HIROSHIMA
Ujina
KURE
TAKAMATSU
MARUGAME
11th Divn
FUSAN
MASAMPO
MOKPO
TSU-SHIMA
Straits of Korea
MOJI
12th Divn
FUKUOKA
OITA
SASEBO
OMURA
KUMAMOTO
NAGASAKI
6th Divn

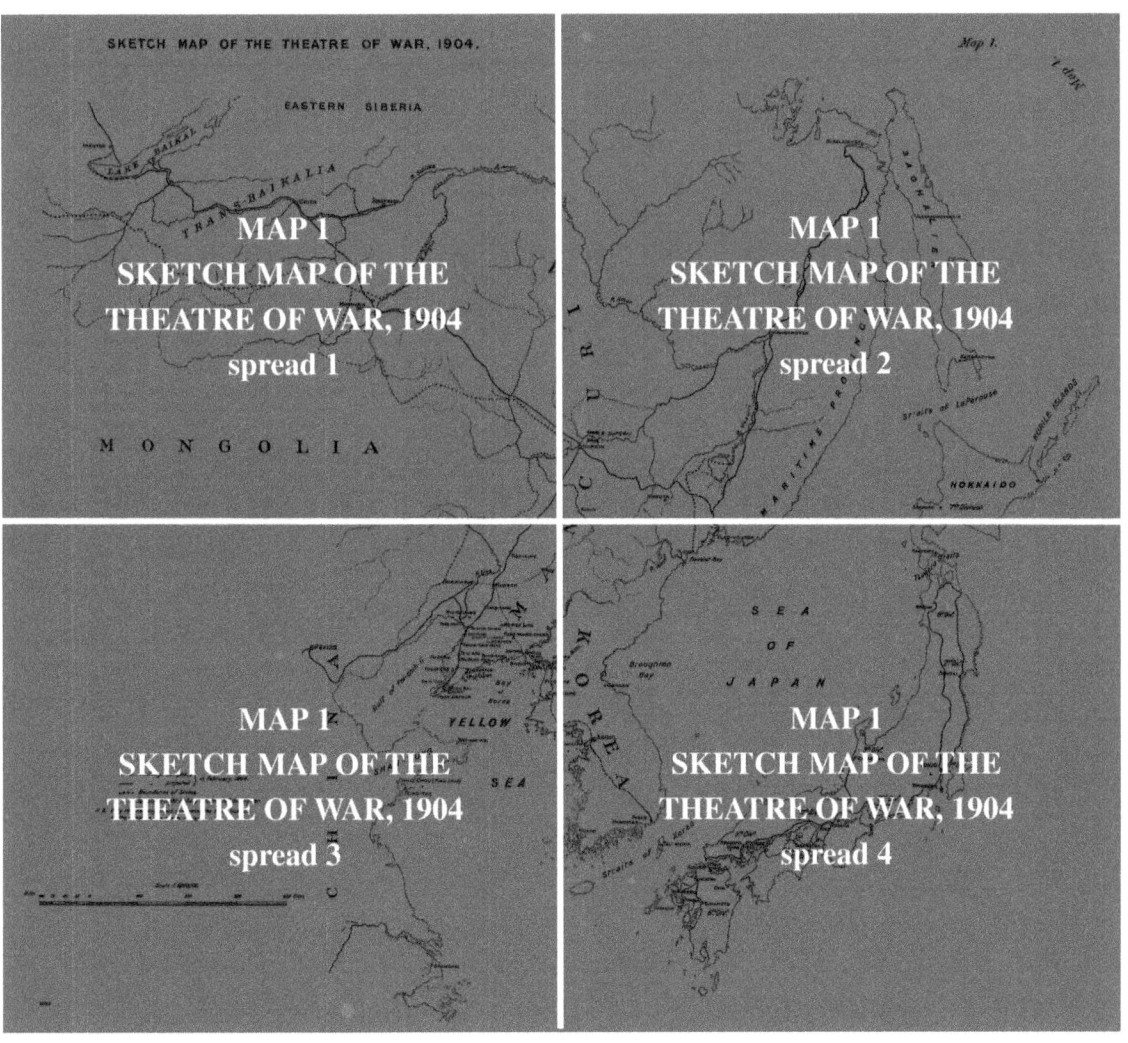

SKETCH MAP OF

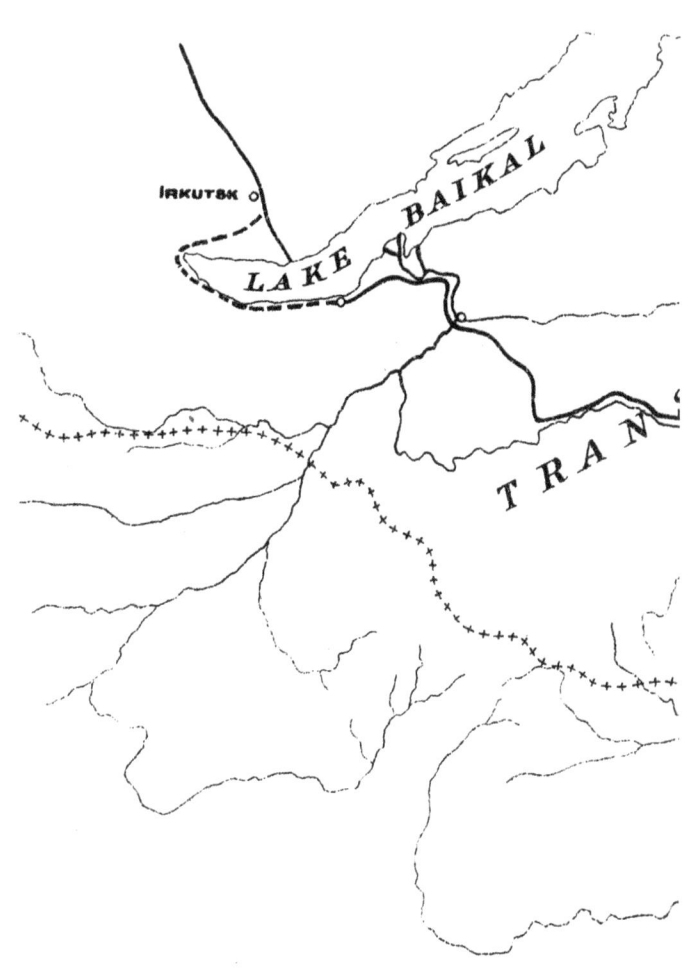

MONG

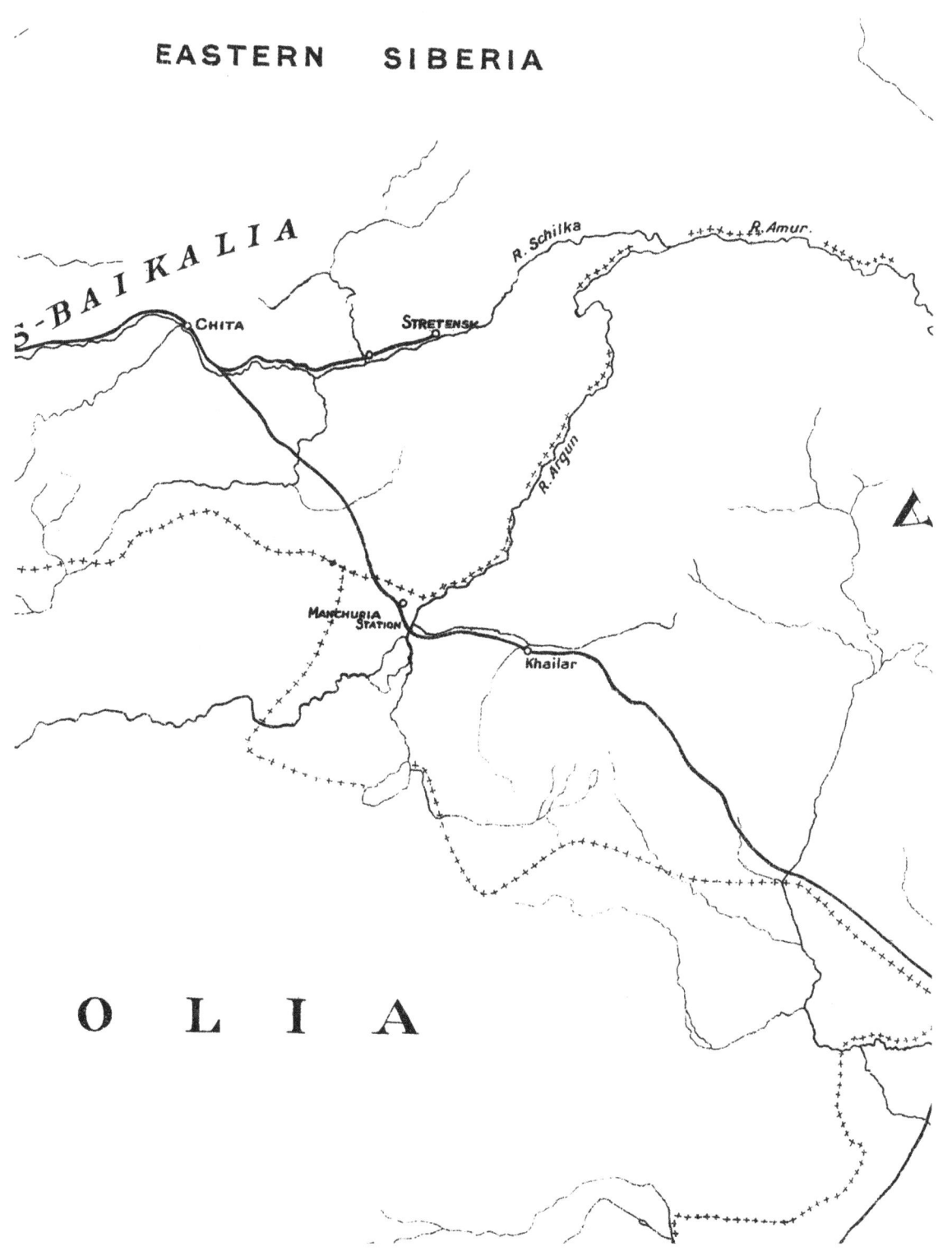

Spread 2

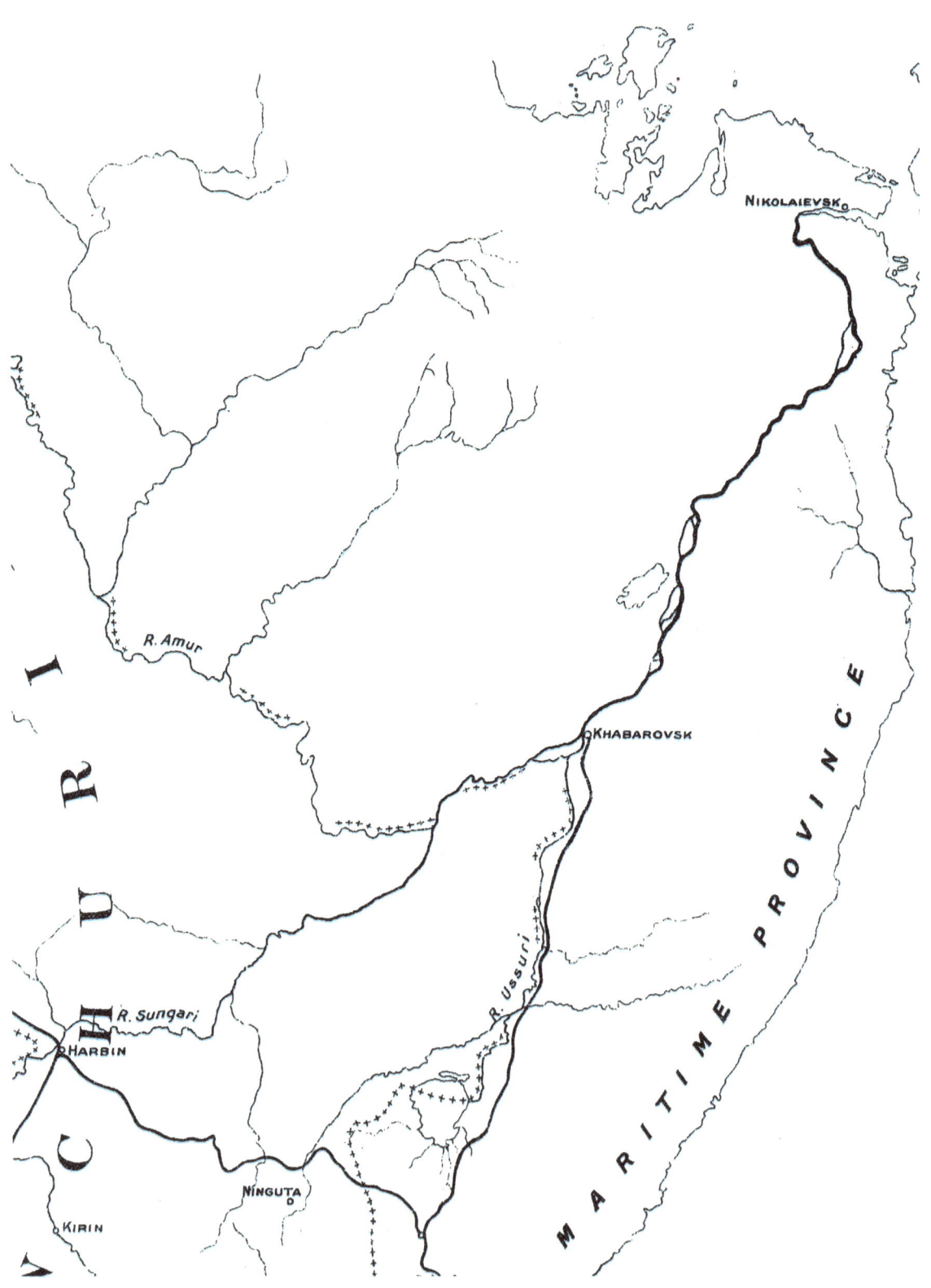

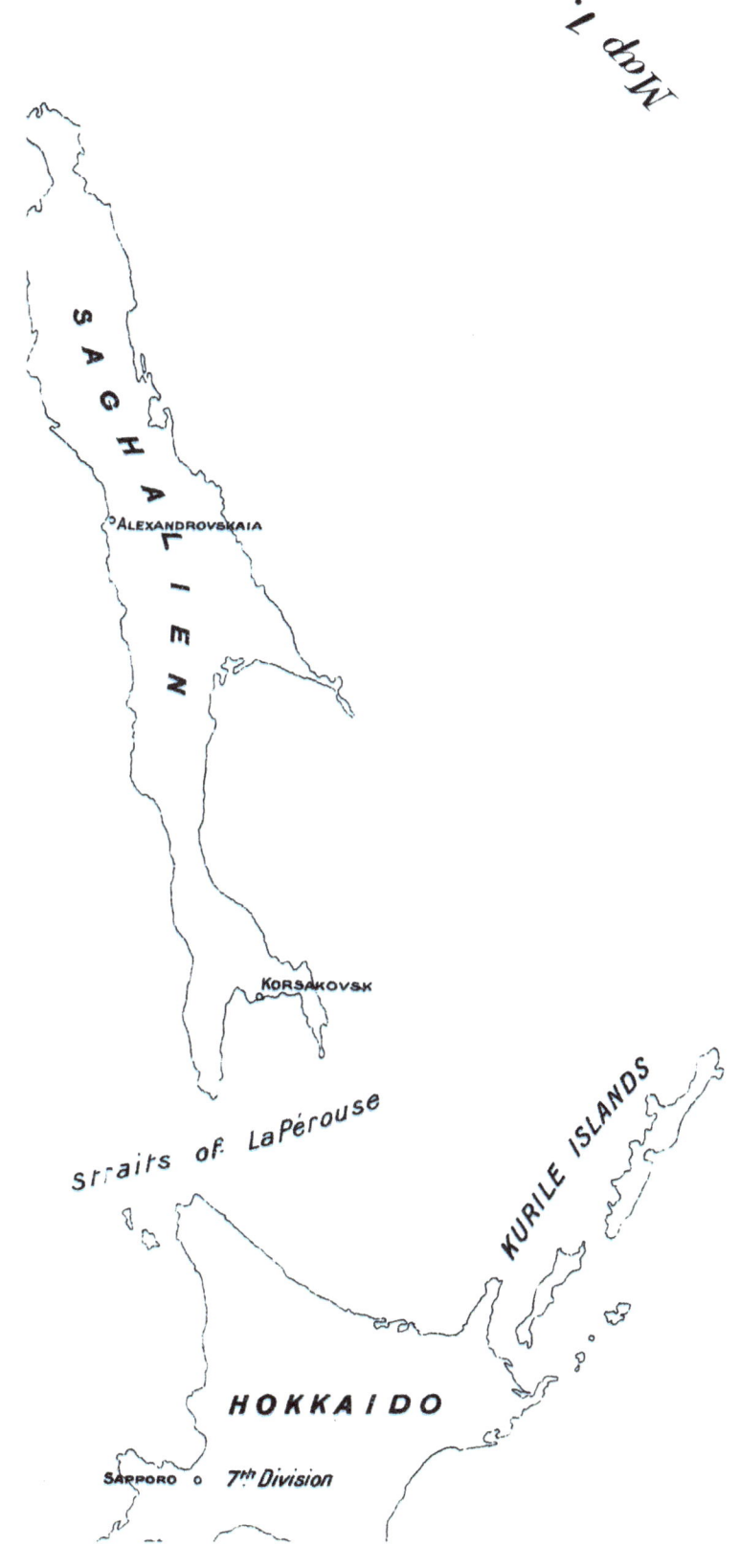

Spread 3

——— Railways completed ⎫ in February, 1...
— — —   " projected ⎭
+-+-+ Boundaries of States.
·········· Japanese light railway constructed du...

N. B. Only the Railway Lines connecting the Head-Qua...
of the Divisions are shown in Japan.

Scale : 1 : 6,000,000.

Miles 100 75 50 25 0   100   200   3...

Spread 4

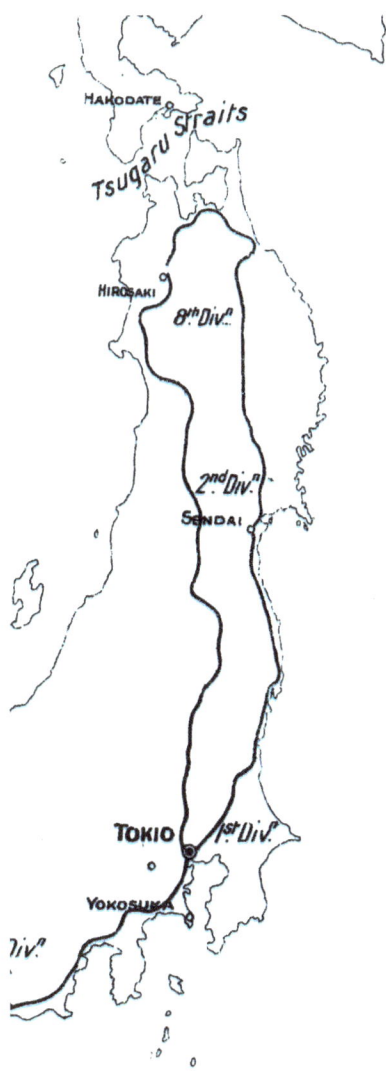

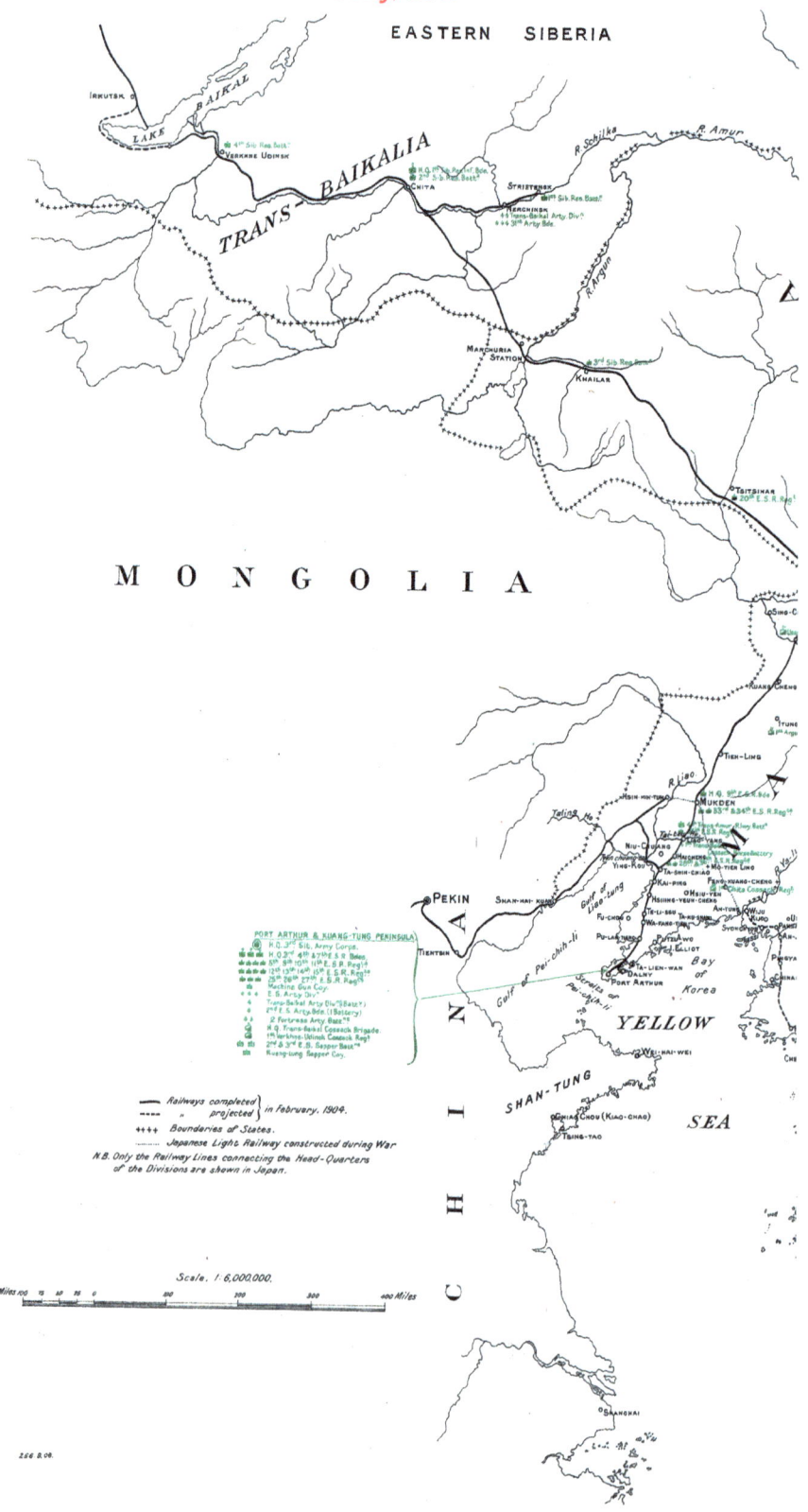

SKETCH MAP OF THE THEATRE OF WAR
Showing the positions of Russian and Japanese Forces at the beginning of February, 1904.

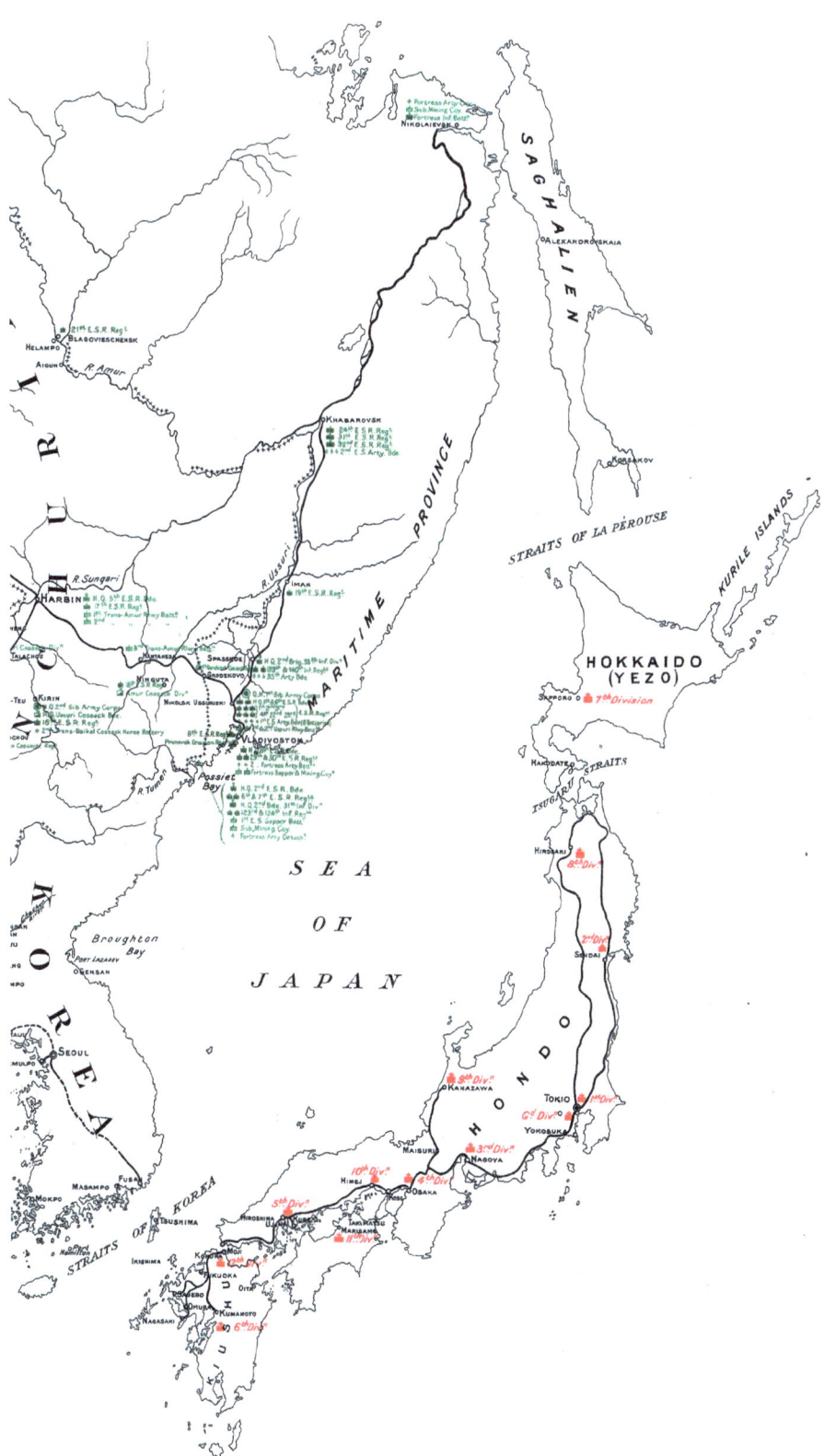

MAP I.

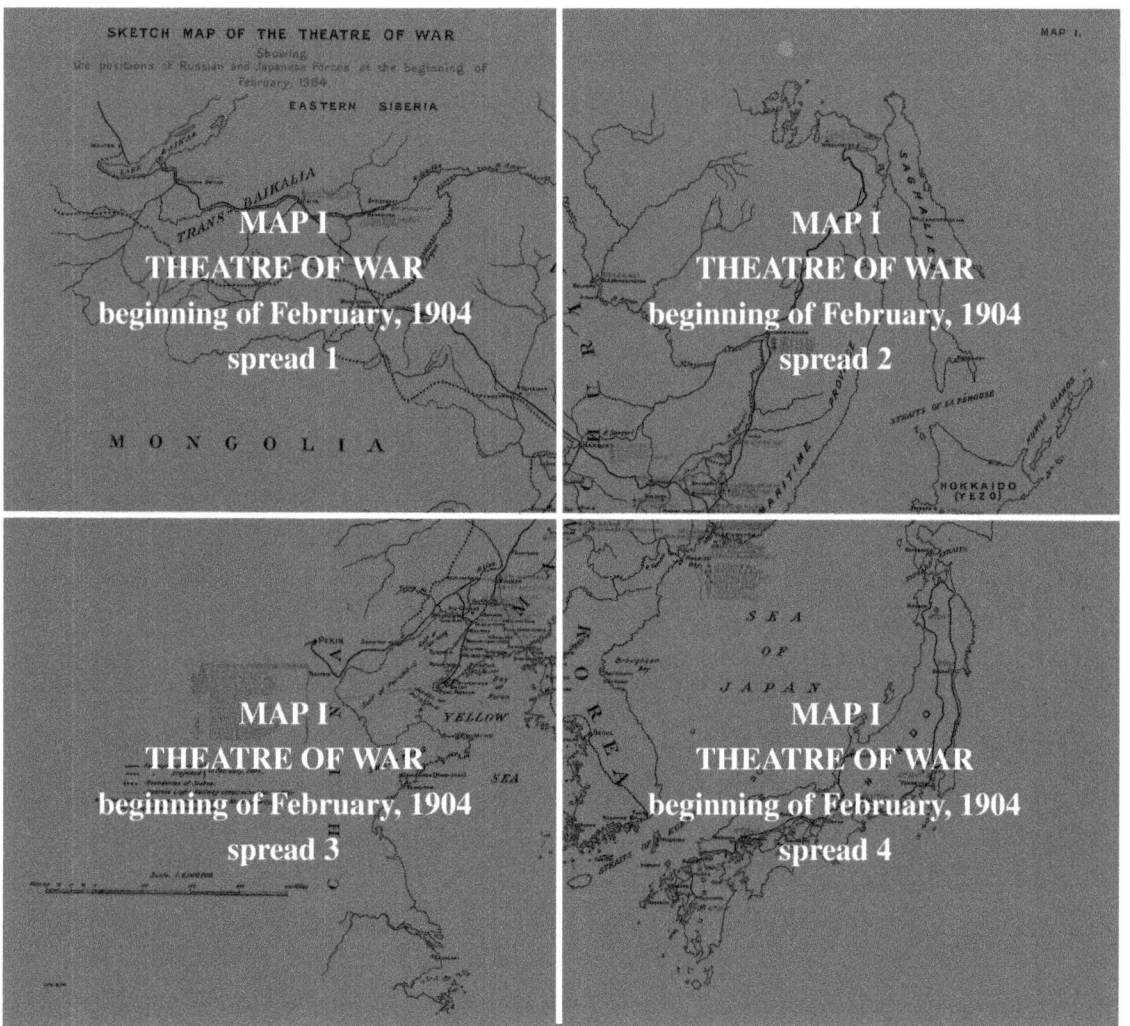

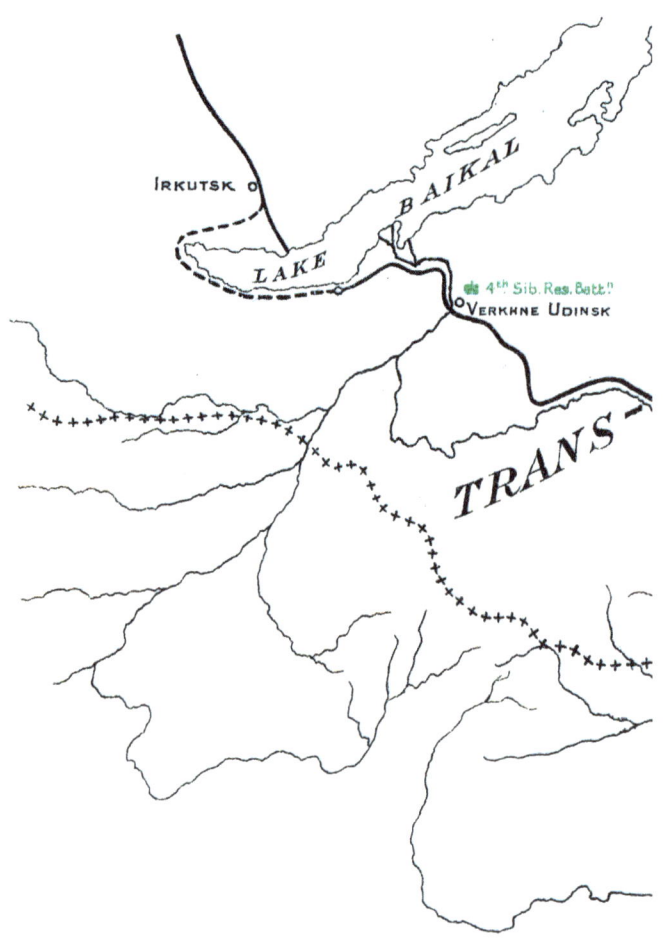

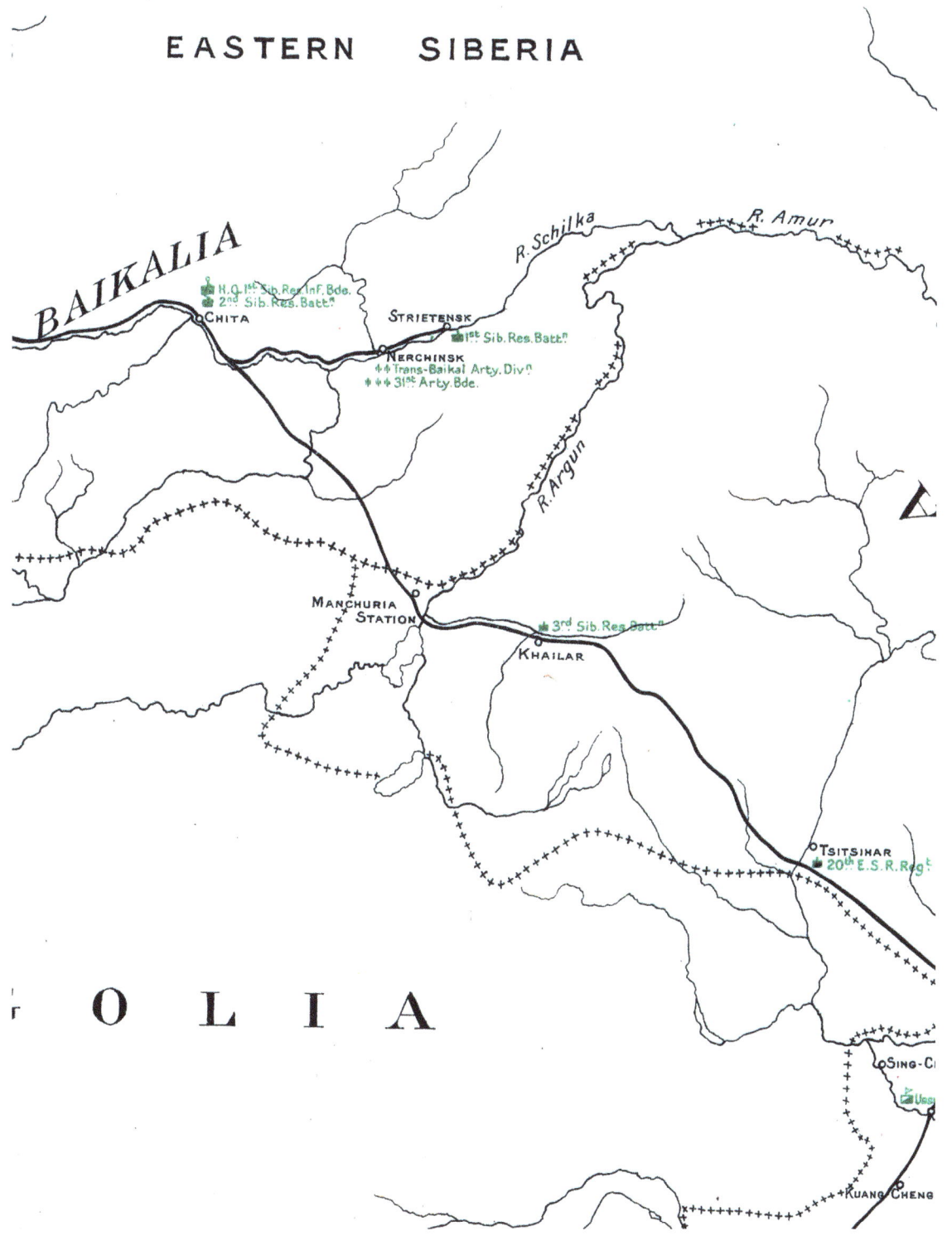

Spread 2

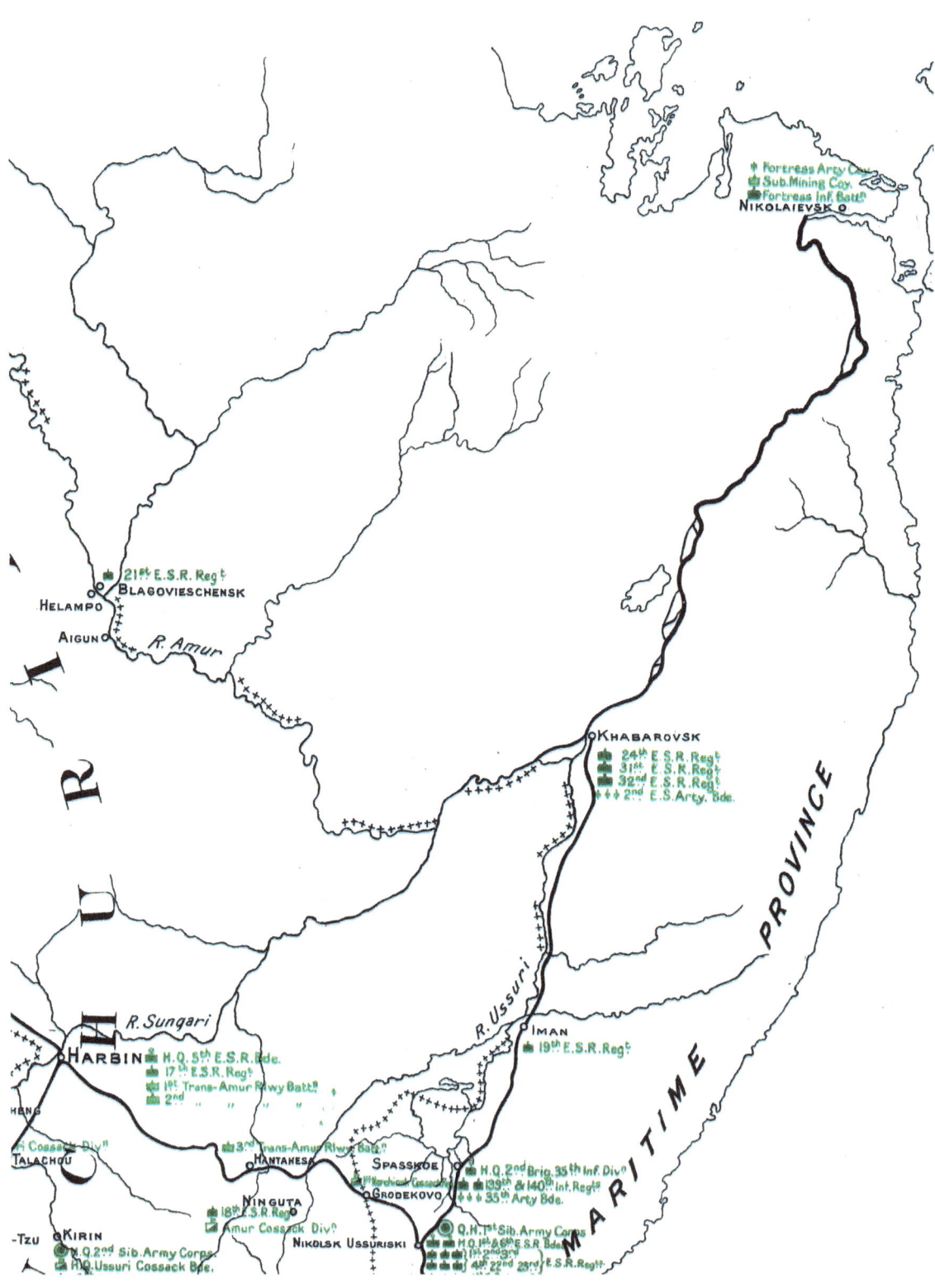

MAP I.

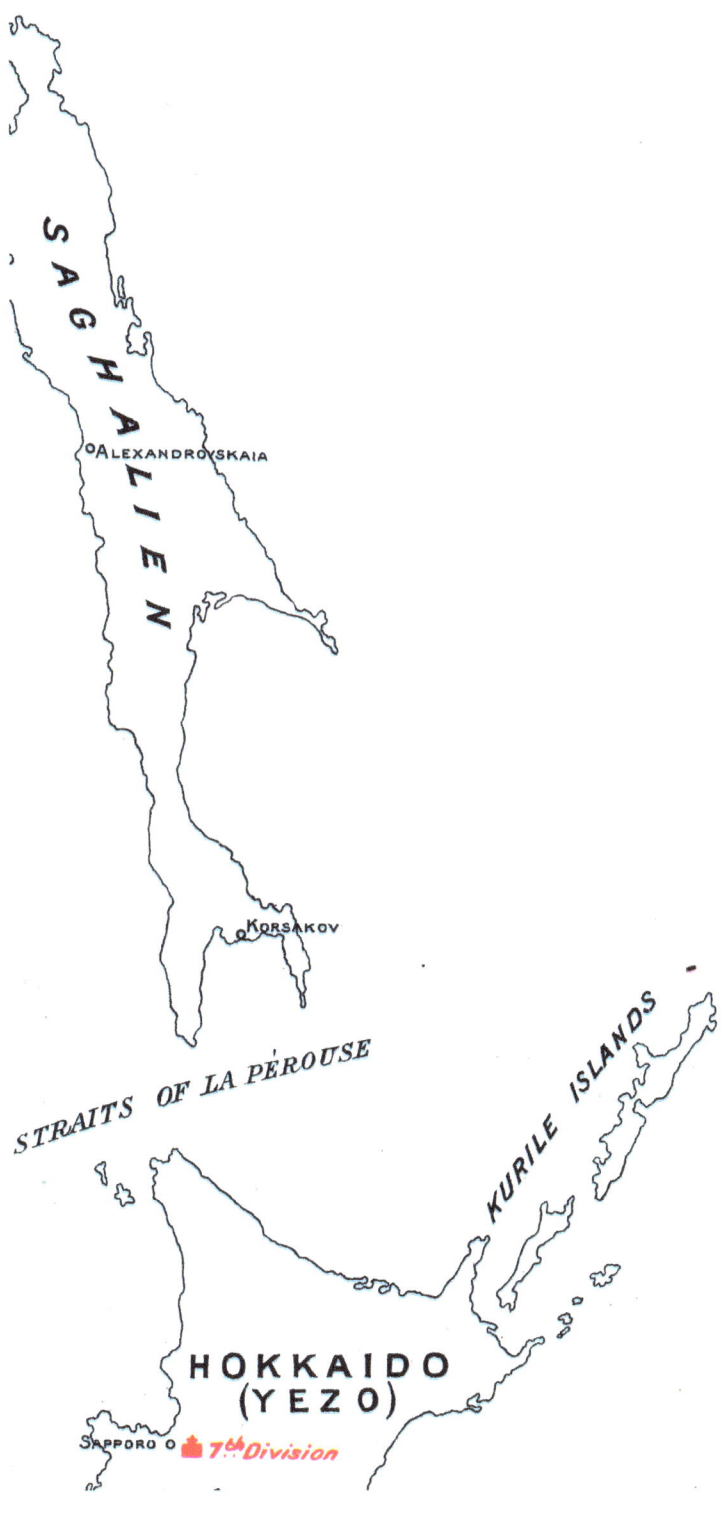

PORT ARTHUR
H.Q. 3rd Si
H.Q.3rd 4t
5th 9th 10t
12th 13th 14
25th 26th 2
Machine Gu
E.S. Arty
Trans-Baikal
2nd E.S. Art
2 Fortress
H.Q. Trans-
1st Verkhne-
2nd & 3rd E.
Kuang-tung

——— Railways completed ⎱ in Februa
---- " projected ⎰
++++ Boundaries of States.
.... Japanese Light Railway cons.
N.B. Only the Railway Lines connecting the He
of the Divisions are shown in Japan.

Scale, 1:6,000,000.
Miles 100 75 50 25 0   100   200

Spread 3

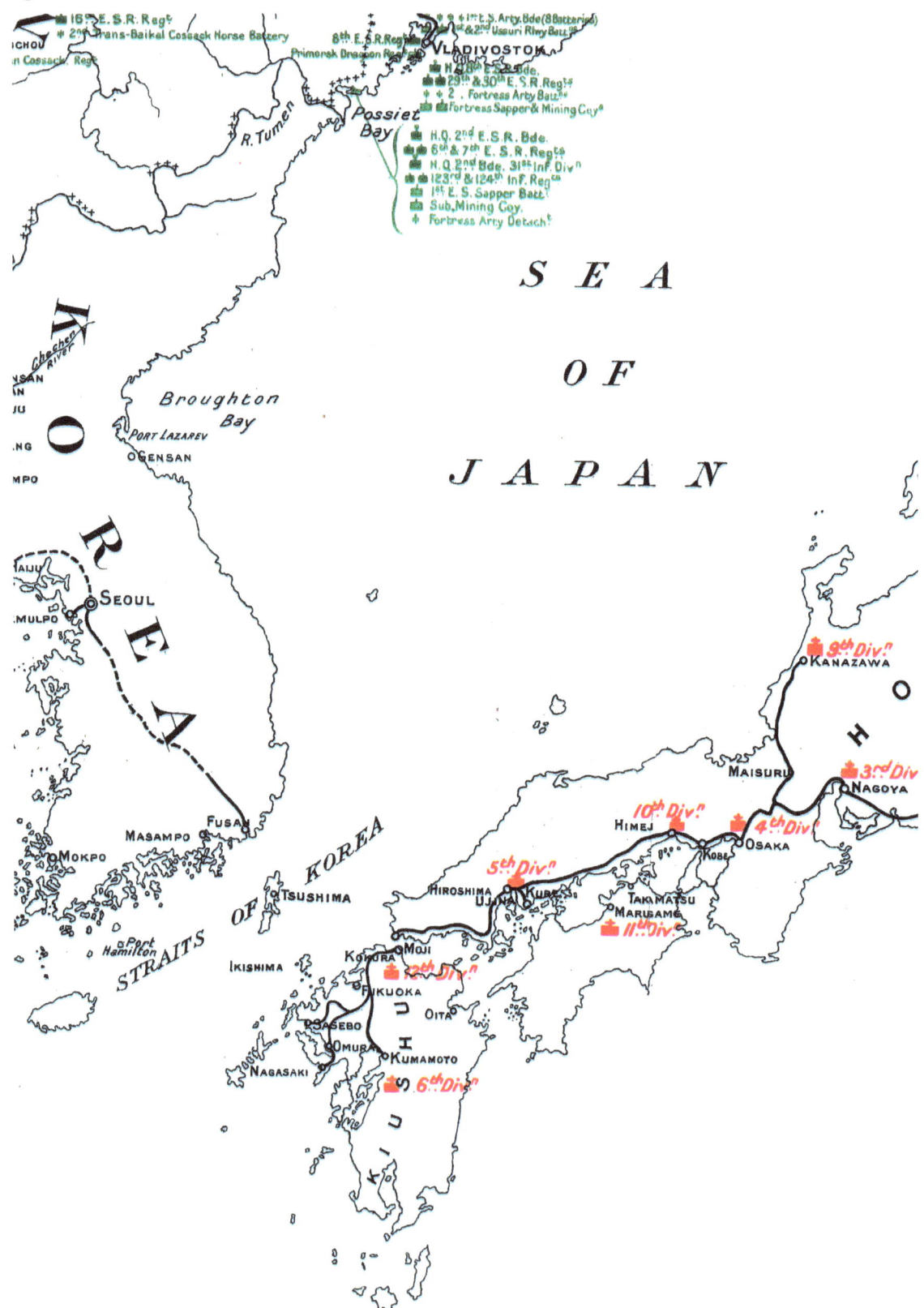

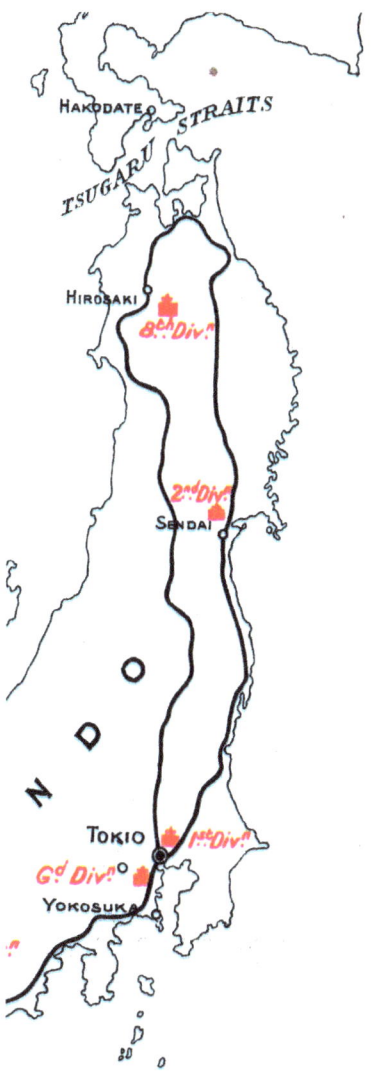

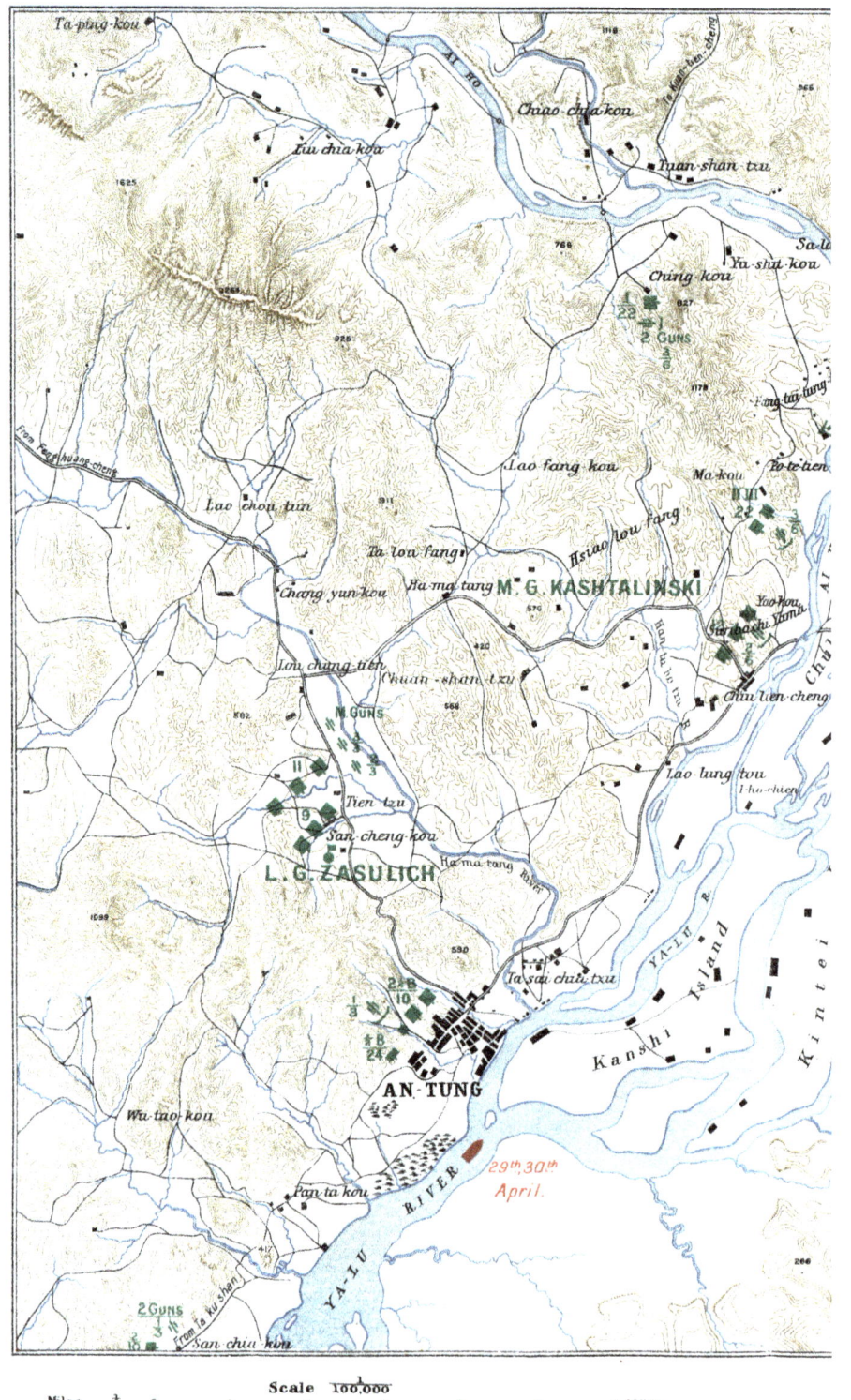

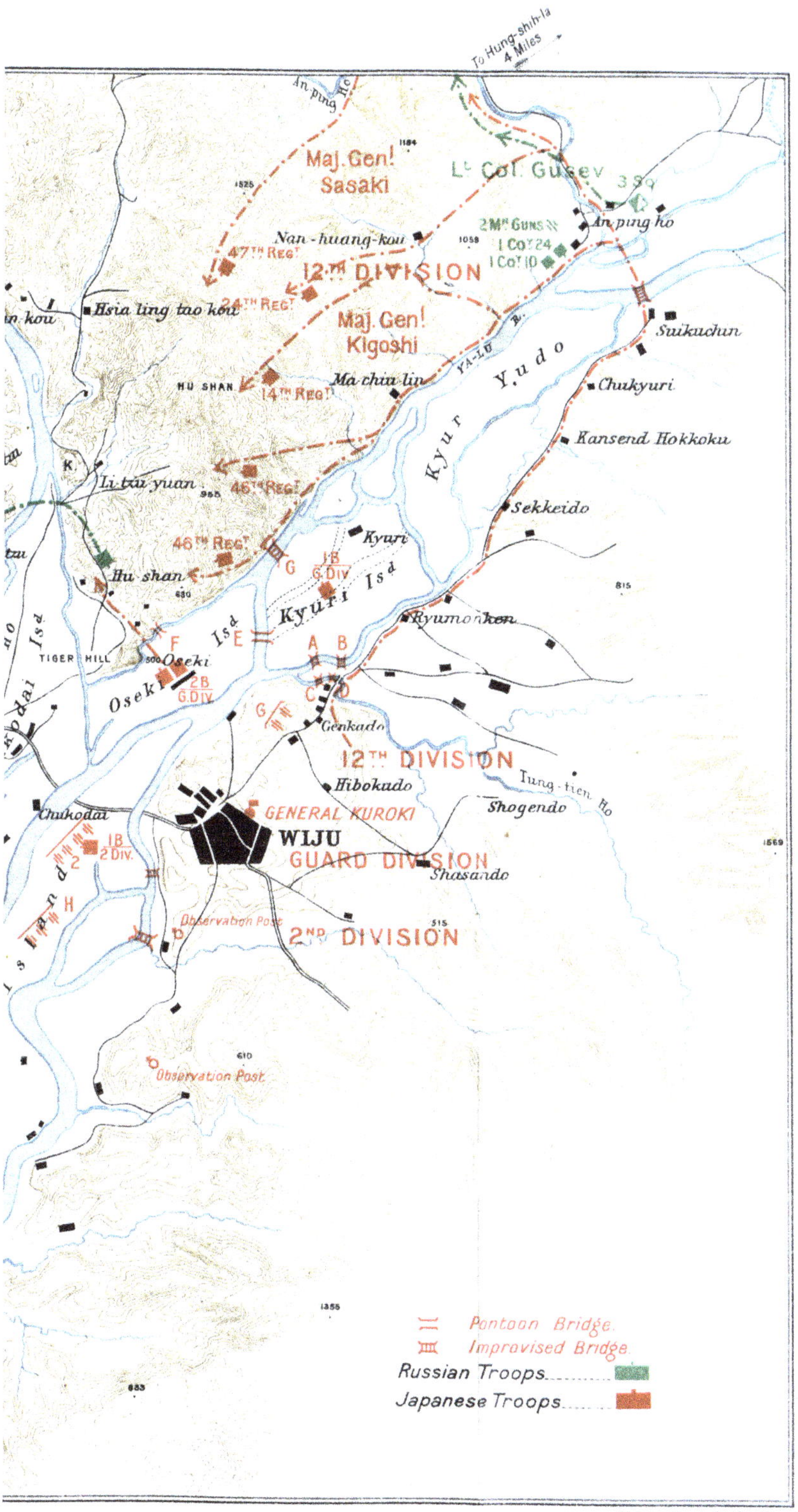

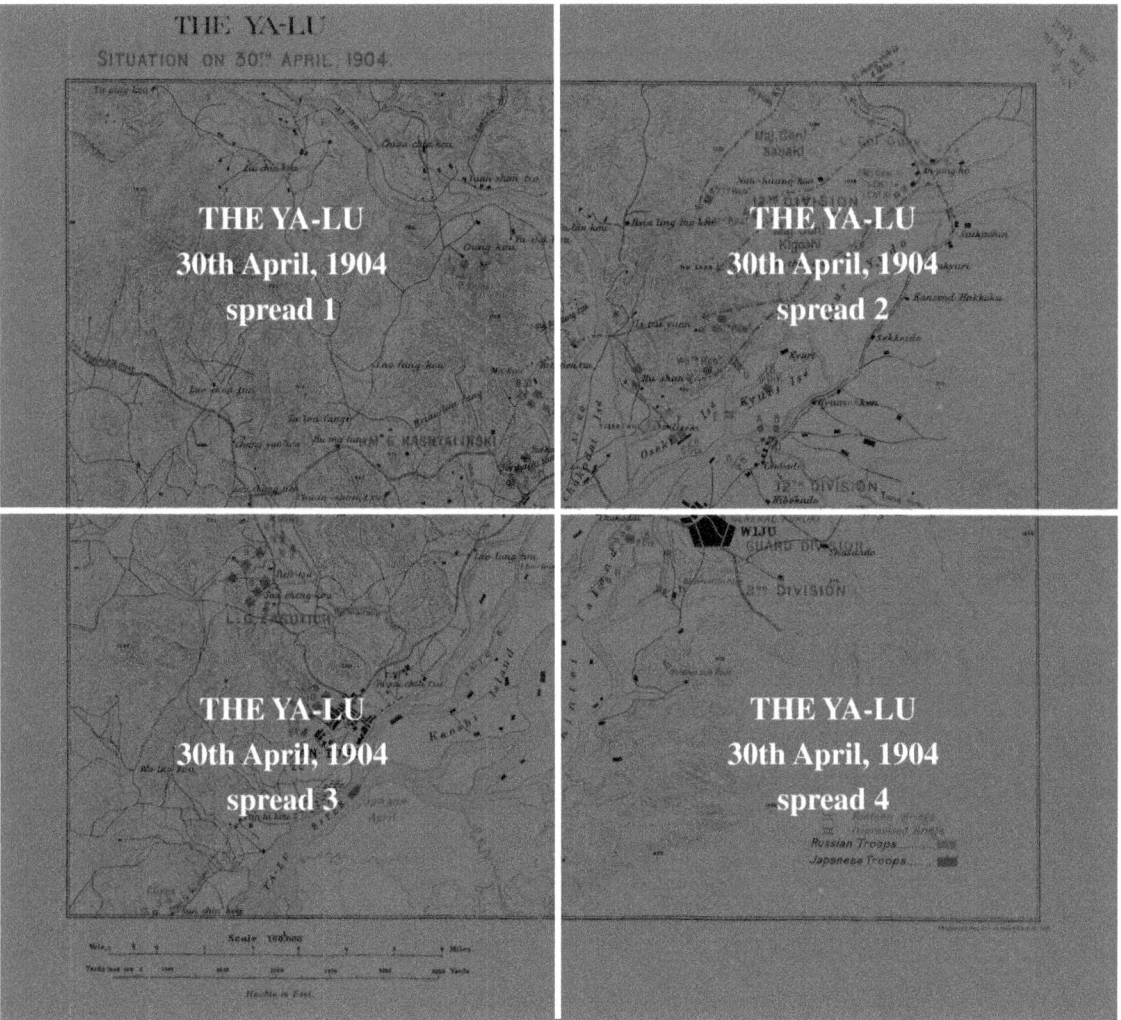

THE

SITUATION ON

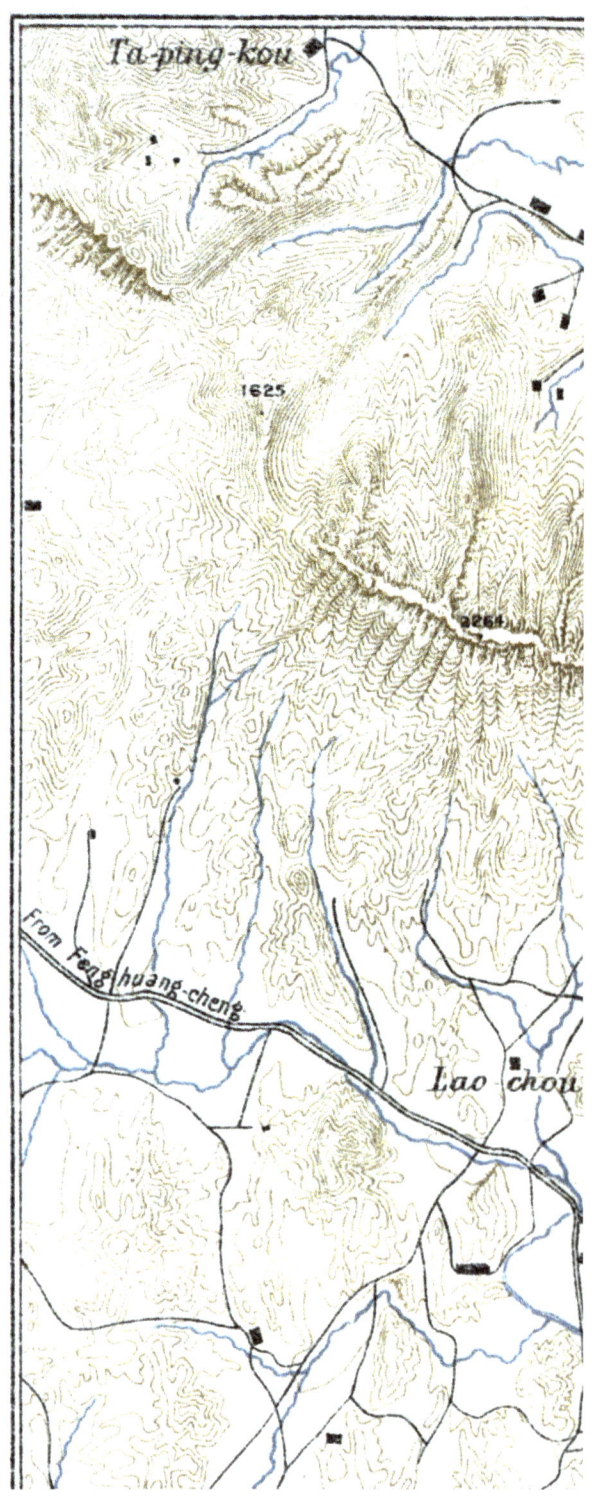

YA-LU
30TH APRIL, 1904.

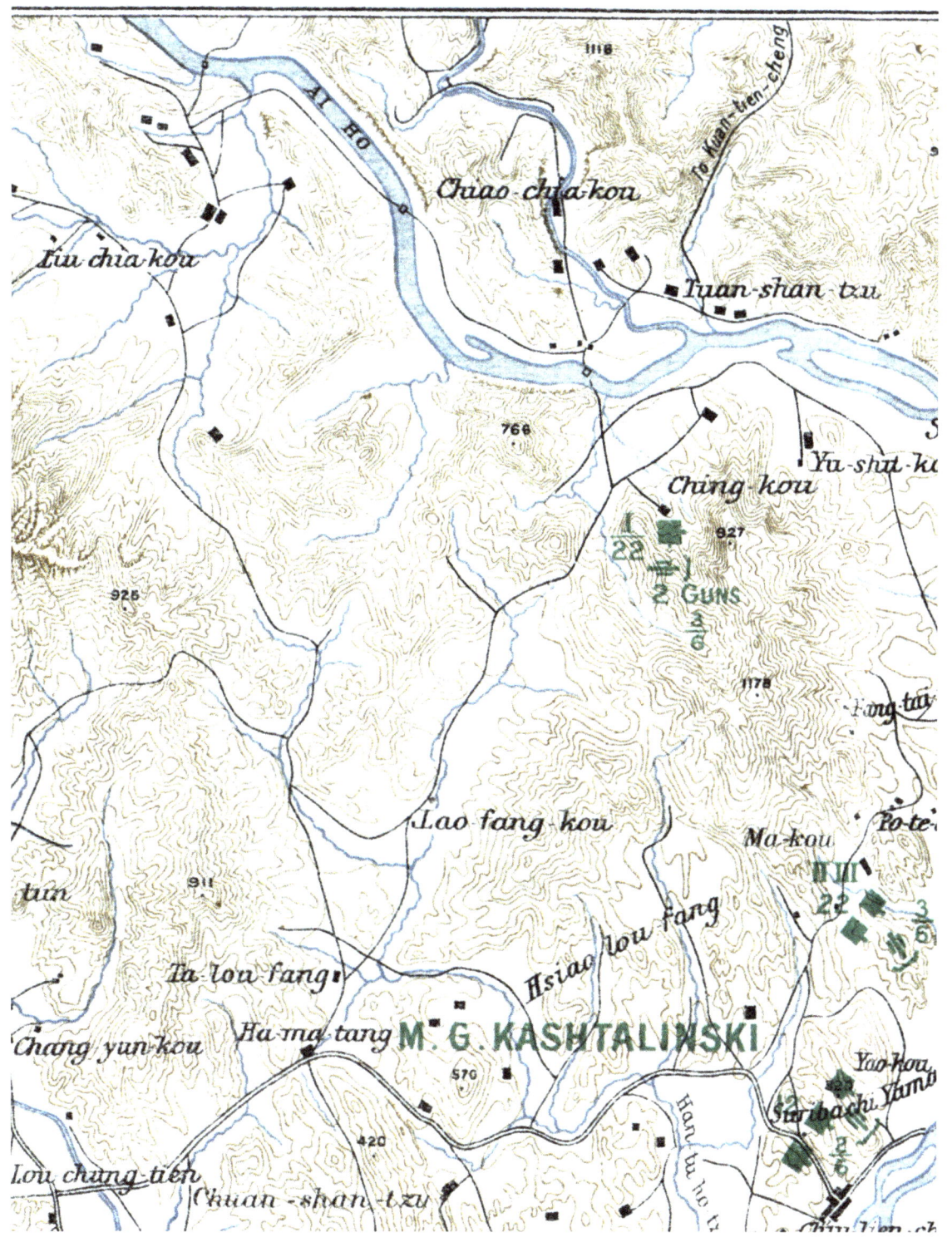

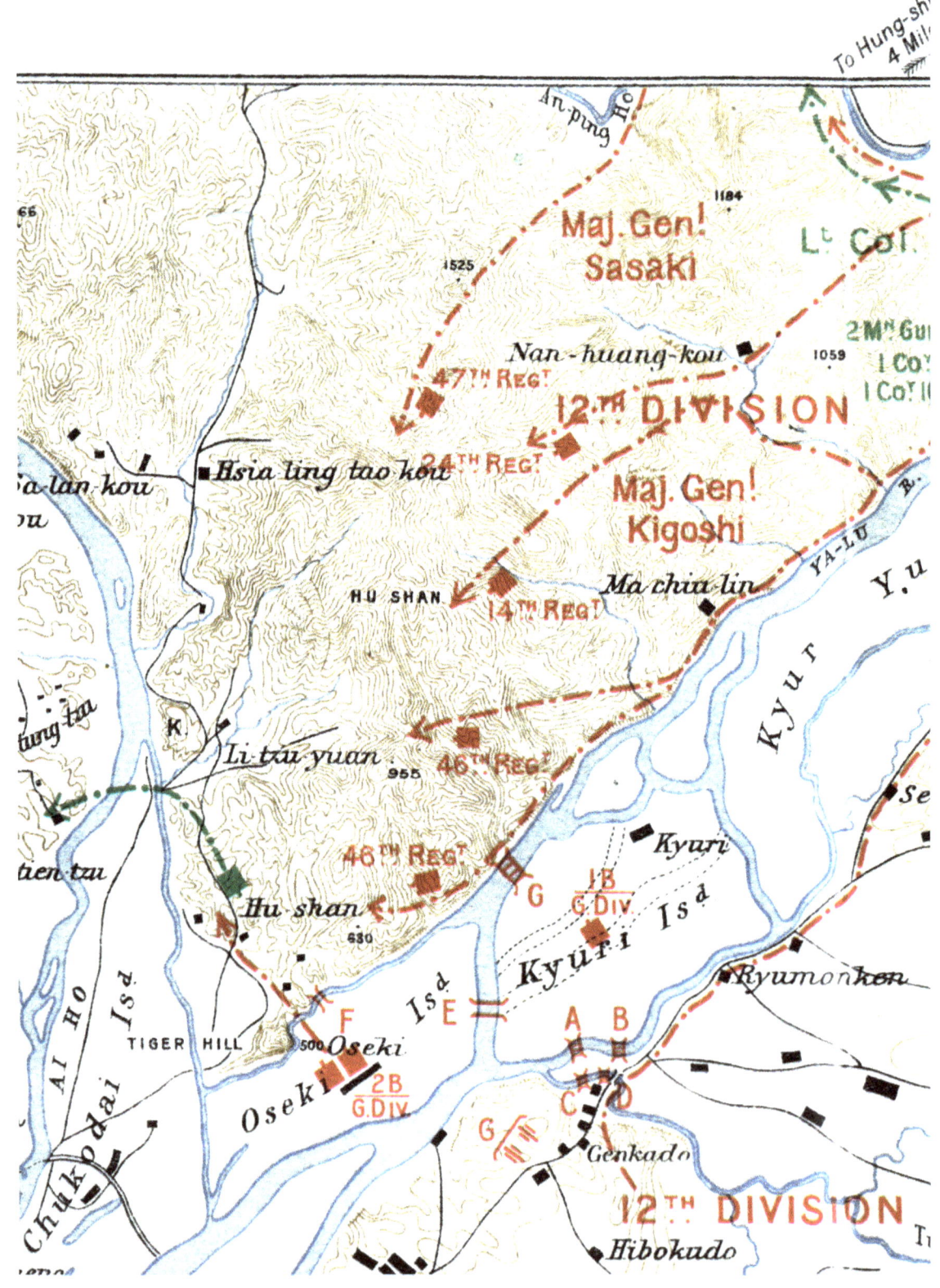

No. 1.
The Ya-lu.
30th April.

Spread 3

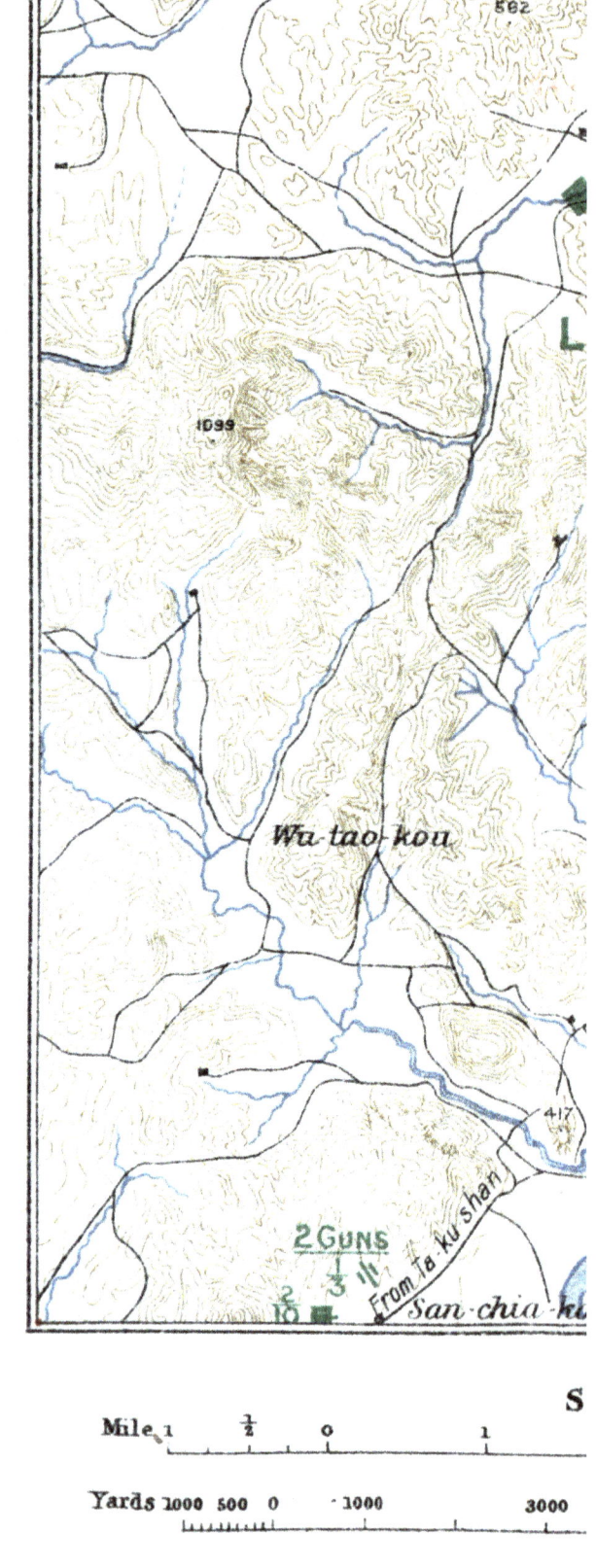

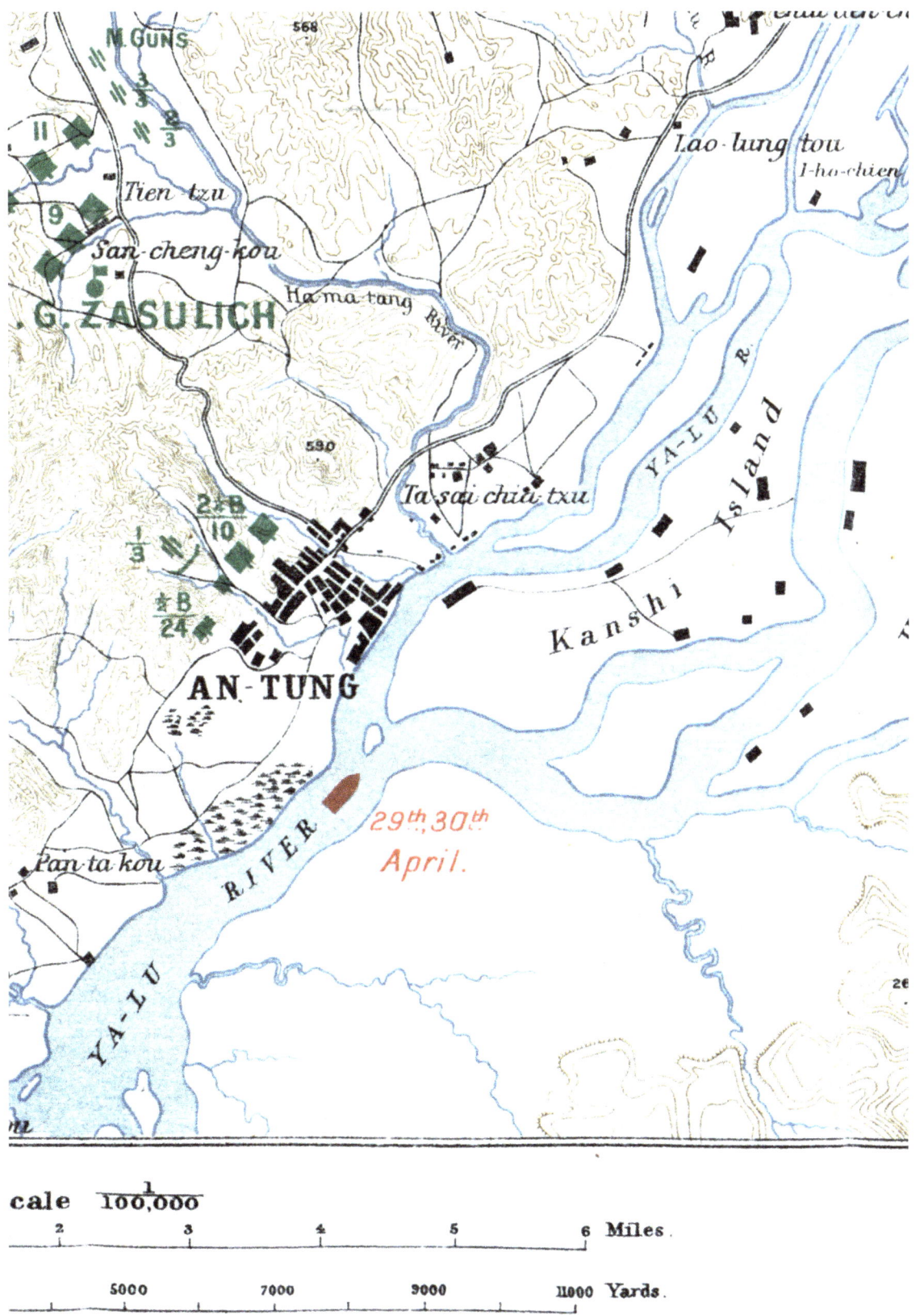

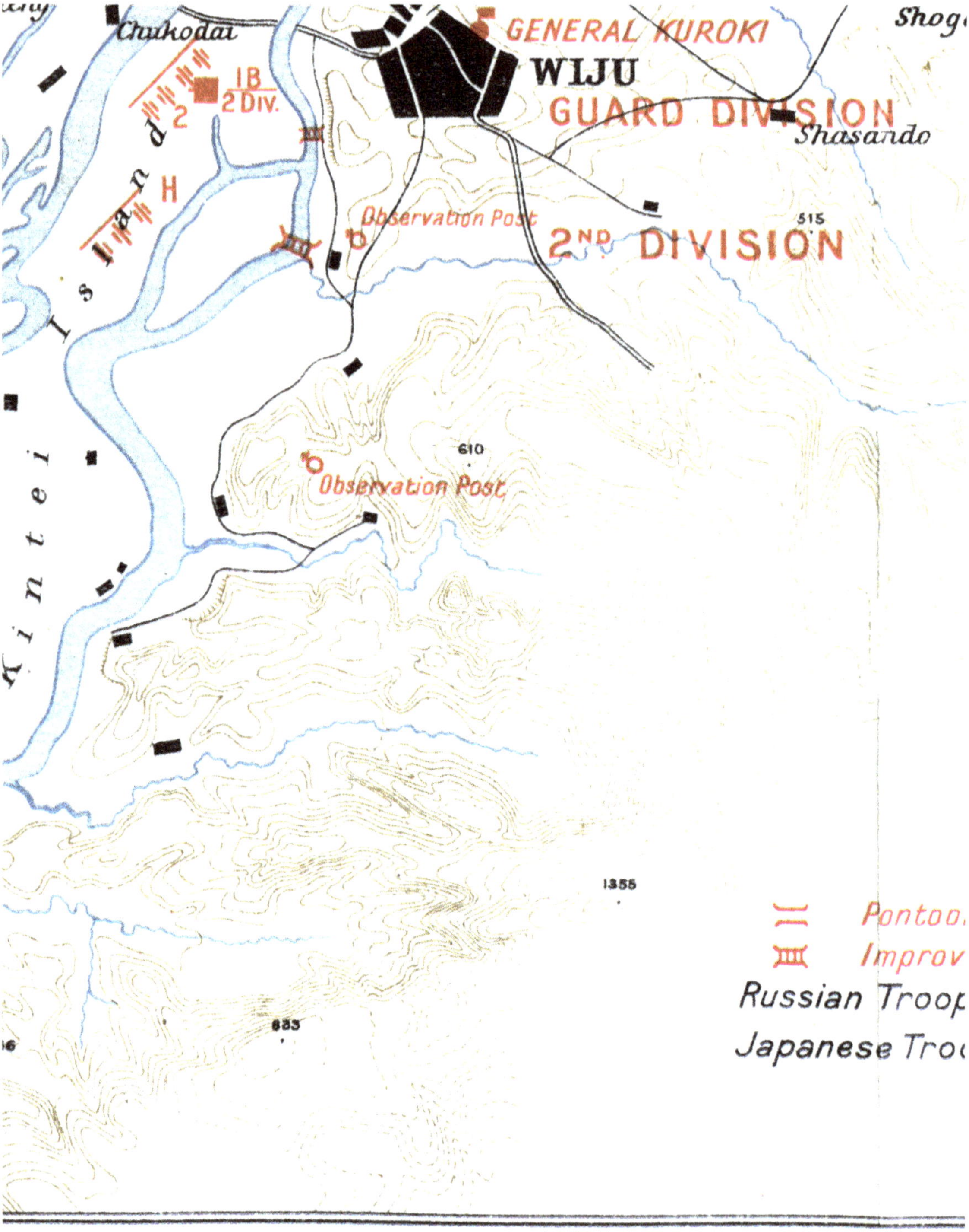
Chukodai
GENERAL KUROKI
WIJU
1B
2 DIV.
2
H
GUARD DIVISION
Shasando
Shog
Island
Observation Post
2ND DIVISION
515
610
Observation Post
Kintei
1355
883
Pontoo
Improv
Russian Troop
Japanese Troo

SITUATION ON 1ST MAY, 1904.

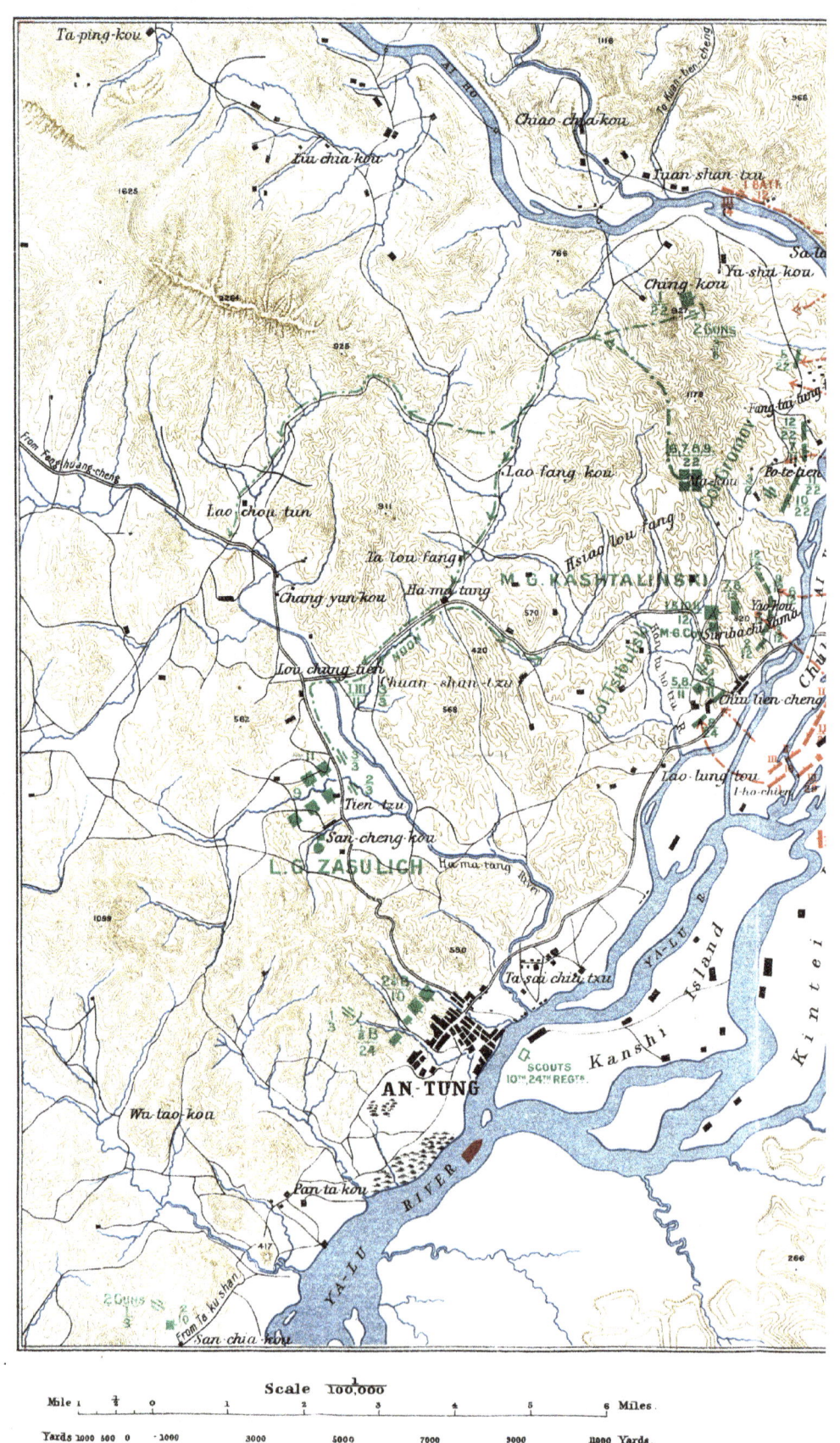

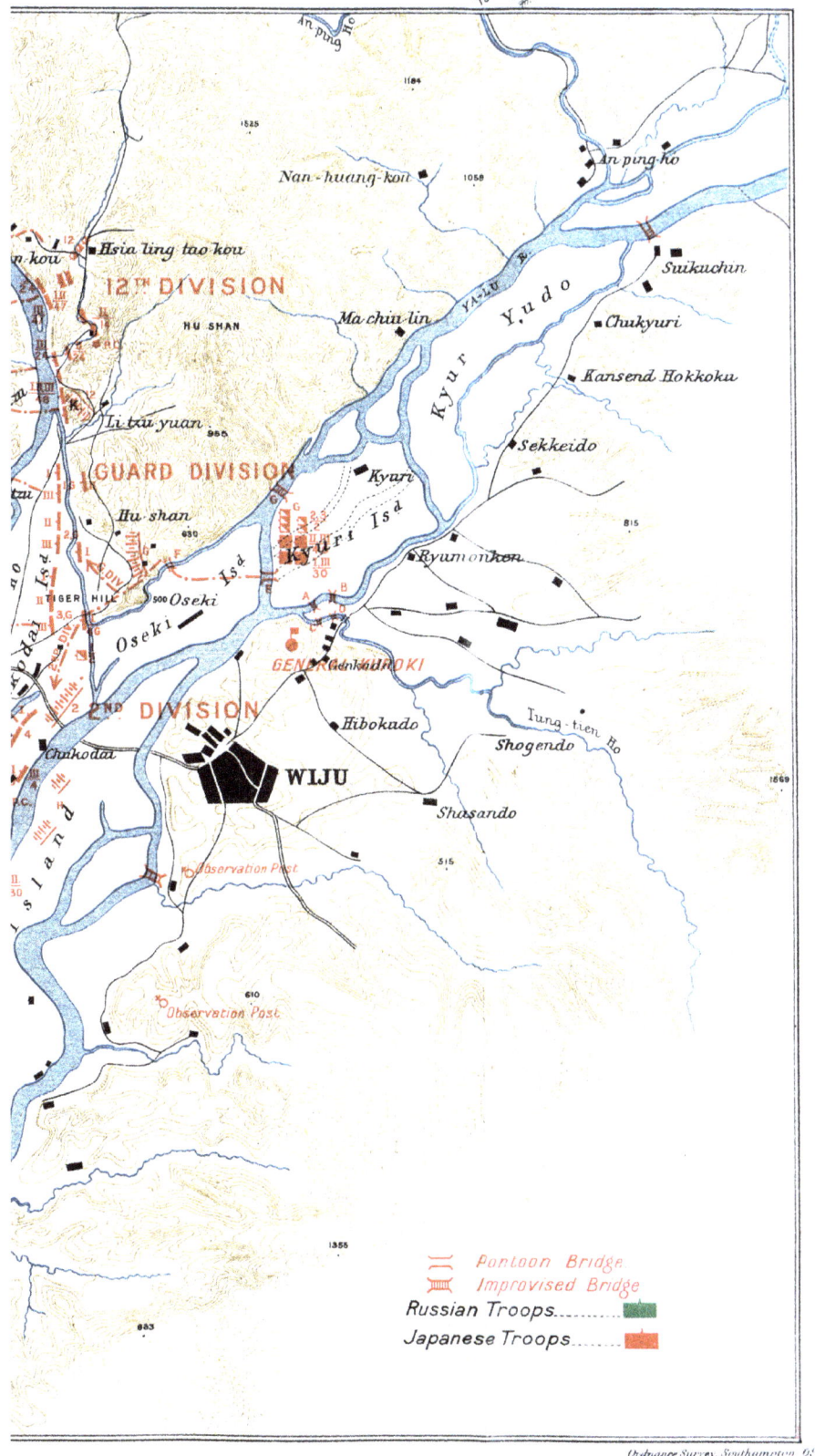

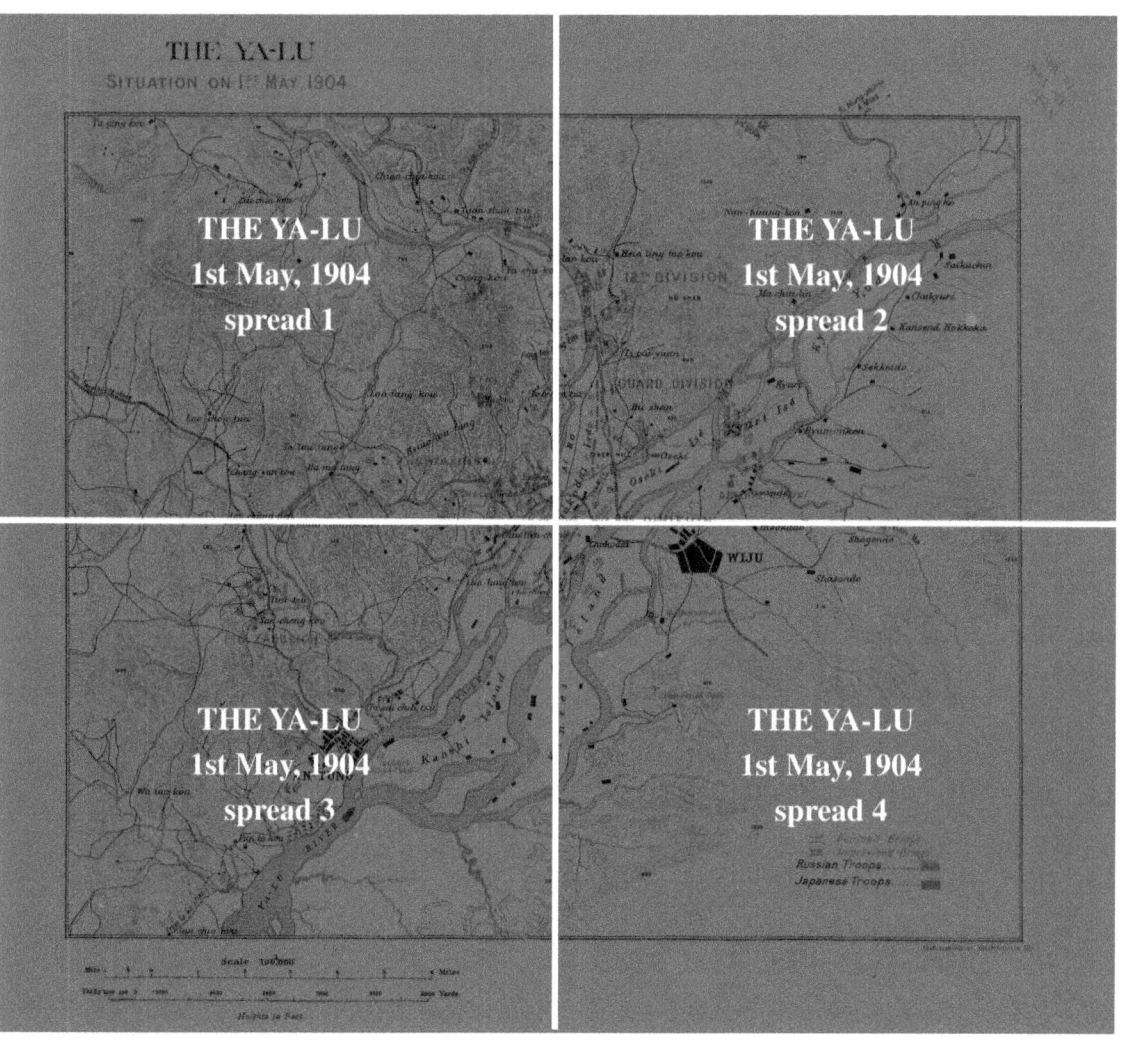

THE
SITUATION ON

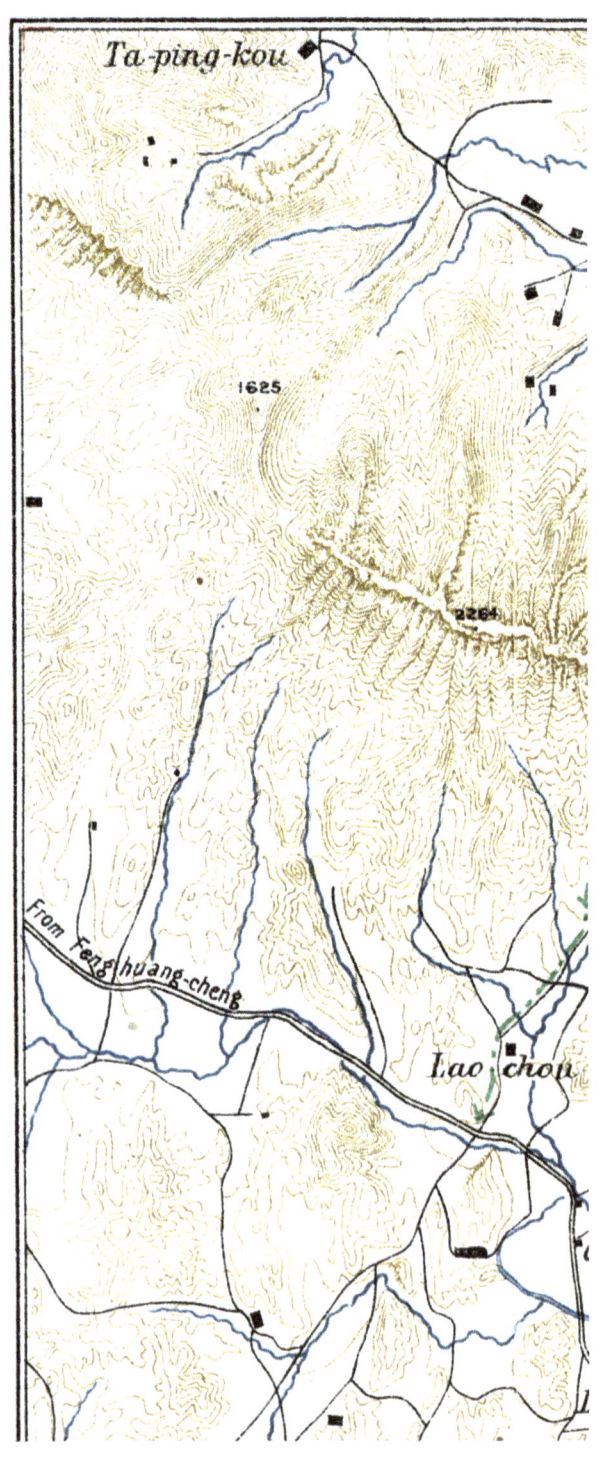

YA-LU
1ST MAY, 1904.

Spread 2

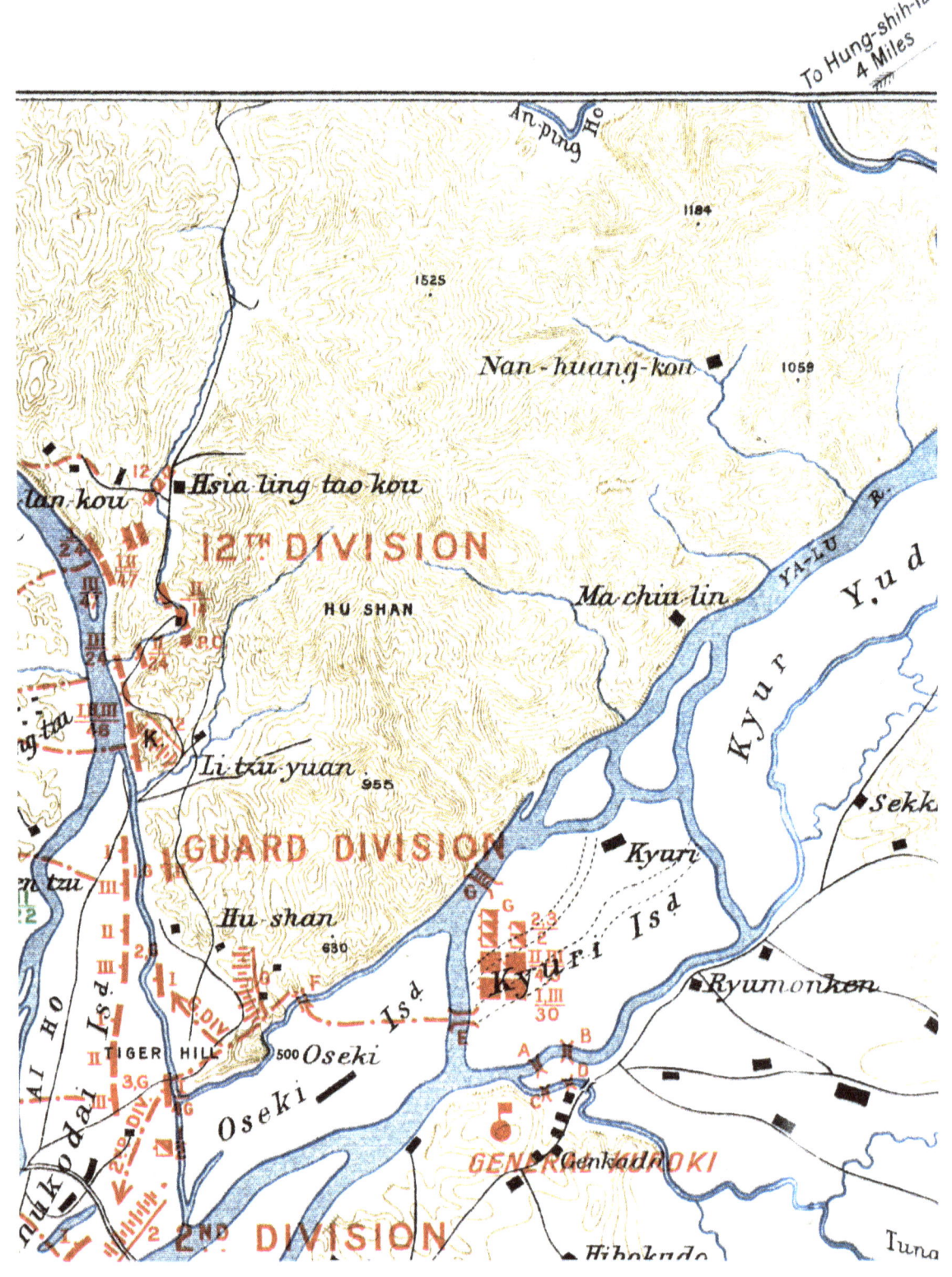

Spread 3

562
1099
Wa-tao-kou
417
2 GUNS
From Ta-ku-shan
San-chia-ko
Sc
Mile 1 ½ 0 1
Yards 1000 500 0 1000 3000

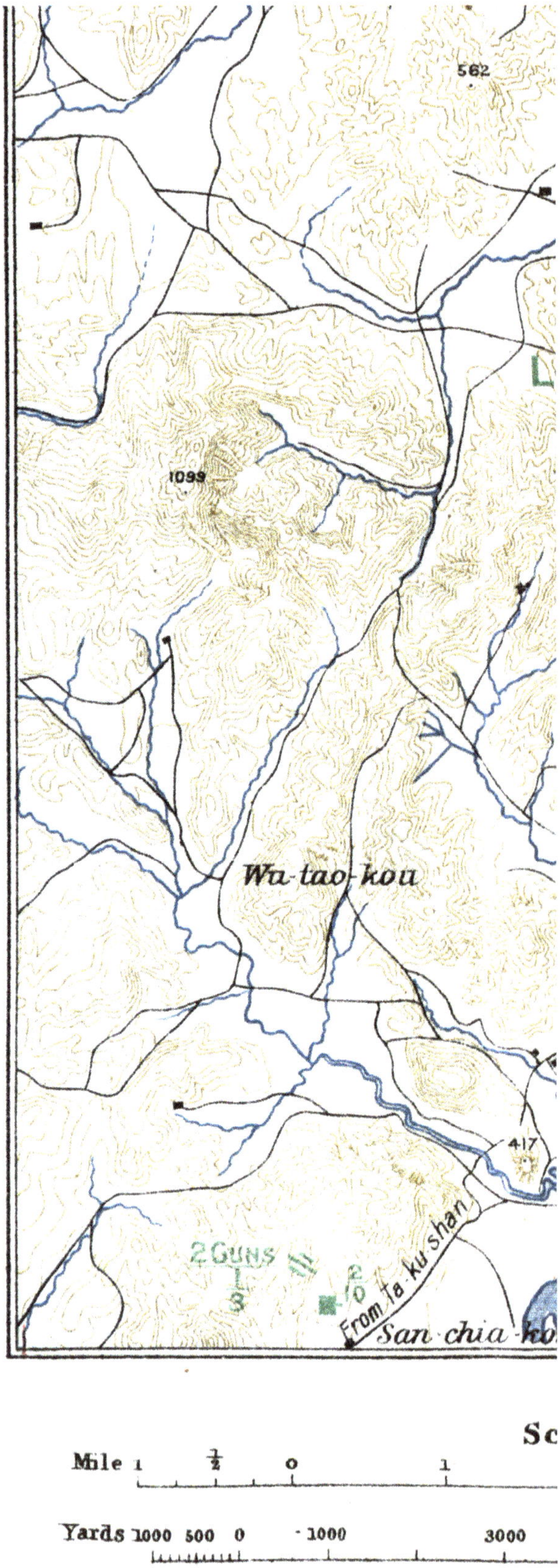

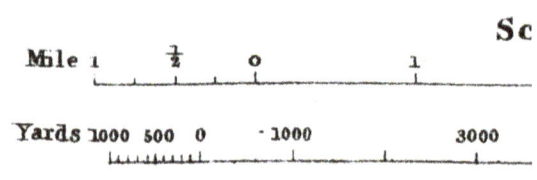

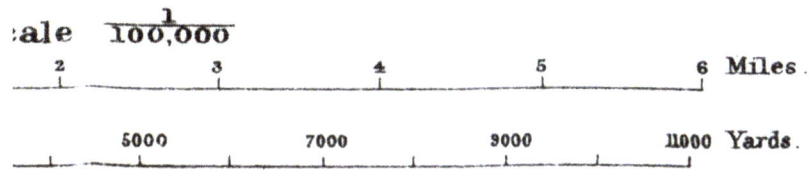

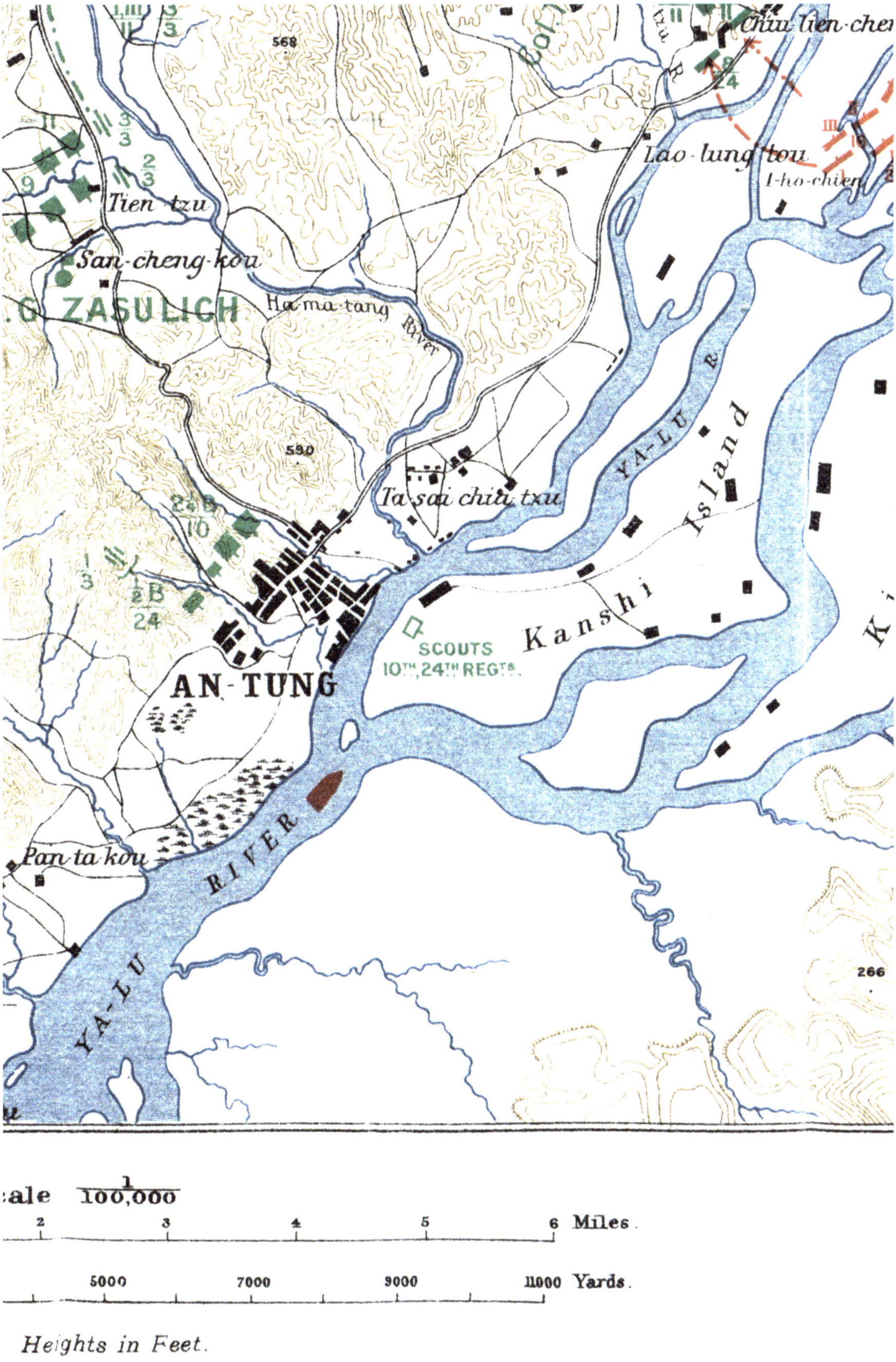

Scale 1/100,000

Heights in Feet.

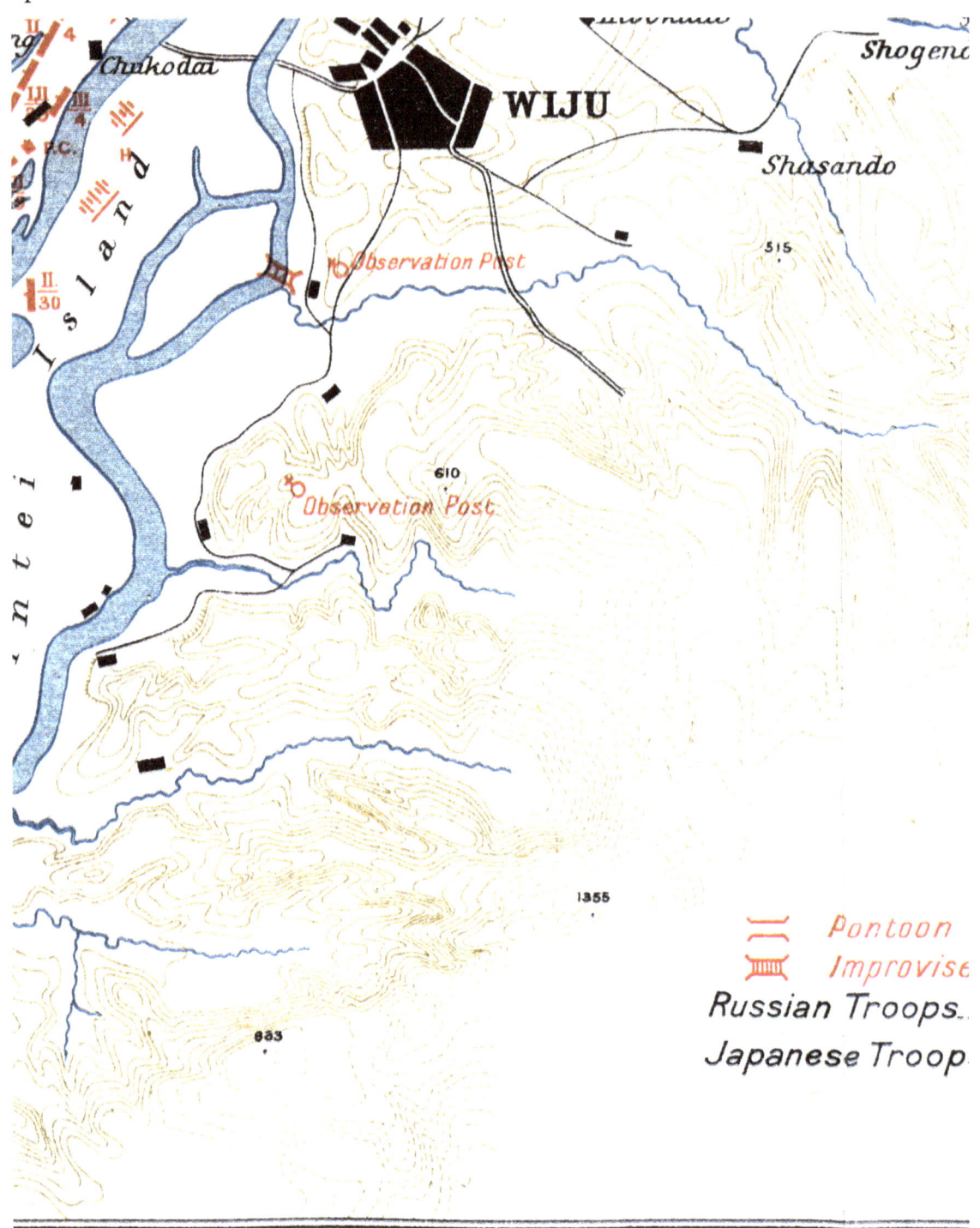

Ordnance Survey, Southampton 0.9.

(Wt. 19634—62 2000 11 | 09—H & S 4718)

www.ingramcontent.com/pod-product-compliance
Lightning Source LLC
Chambersburg PA
CBHW061124010526
44114CB00029B/3002